TAKASHI AMANO

NATURE AQUARIUM

COMPLETE WORKS

ガラスの中の大自然

1985-2009

Prologue

Looking back the 30 years of Nature Aquarium

● The years since the birth of Nature Aquarium

It was about 30 years ago when I created a full-fledged Iwagumi layout for the first time. It was a layout created in a 120 cm aquarium, and it was arranged with river rocks and planted with *Echinodorus tenellus*, which had just been introduced in Japan. The aquascape, which looked like grasslands with schooling *Paracheirodon axelrodi*, was well received by my family and friends. Although the name "Nature Aquarium" did not exist yet, I believe that this was the very first work of mine that led to my current layout style. Although I was already researching a substrate specialized for growing aquatic plants, from then on I devoted myself to developing dependable systems to grow healthy aquatic plants. This resulted in liquid fertilizers, a CO_2 injection system, and lighting improvements, and I produced many layouts along the way. These layouts were published in aquarium magazines at that time and the name, "Nature Aquarium," started to catch on.

The layouts that were created from the mid 1980s to early 90s were compiled into two photo books, *Nature Aquarium World Book 1*, published in '92, and *Nature Aquarium World Book 2*, published in '94. While the layouts created since the mid 90s have been published in various aquarium magazines, such as the monthly *Aqua Journal*, they have not been compiled into a photo book in Japan (although some of them were published overseas as a photo book). About 15 years have passed since *Nature Aquarium World Book 2* was published. I have received a number of requests for a new photo book from both home and abroad in the past few years. This new photo book has chrono-logically arranged layouts that were carefully selected from all

the existing photographs (positive films) of Nature Aquarium layouts, including those published in the previous two photo books. Printing technology has made great advancements in the last 15 years. All of the images, including those published in the past photo books, were rescanned from the original positive films, and I personally edited the colors for the book. Therefore, I believe that the printed images are a lot clearer and more vivid than the previously published ones, and now viewers can enjoy images that are faithful to the original films. The aquascape data for individual layouts were also revised to include up-to-date nomenclature as much as possible based on the original data.

Upon reviewing the data, you may notice that the equipment being used in the layouts has changed greatly over time. For example, while CO_2 was injected directly into the water flow in the early period, CO_2 is diffused more naturally in recent years, using Pollen Glass in the majority of the aquariums except for in an overflow type aquarium. Similarly, while the majority of the layouts in the first half of the book had light fixtures that housed NA Lamps, the majority in the latter half have light fixtures with green type metal halide lamps. The development of a pendant type light fixture also enabled a new style of expression, such as an open top aquarium. The substrate also changed from those that were composed of primarily marine gravels in the early period to those composed primarily of Aqua Soil in the later period. The change in the substrate materials enabled those aquatic plants that were difficult to grow in Sea Gravel to grow easily and it altered the types of aquatic plants that were used in the layouts as well. The

advancement in equipment and substrate materials influenced the layouts and broadened the range of expressions.

● The reason for my insistence on large format film

Although both the photography world and printing industry have globally gone from being analog to mostly digital over the past 15 years, the photographs in this book were taken with large format film, the ultimate form of analog. Speaking of analog vs. digital, I am a man from the analog era. Since the proliferation of photographs taken with digital cameras, by contrast I believe that some of us have come to appreciate the superior quality of the photographs taken with film. Film has much richer color gradation in particular, and it offers far greater information for green and red colors of aquatic plants, which tend to appear more flat in images from a digital camera. Therefore, film is superior for expressing the three-dimensional quality of aquatic plants. The characteristics of film are reflected in printing through optimal scanning and plate making. As a result, the finished, printed material has richer colors as compared to images taken by a digital camera. Although digital cameras are advancing by leaps and bounds and their resolutions and sensitivities are greatly increasing, film cameras still seem to have an edge on them in terms of color gradation. They won't be able to surpass 8 x 20 and 11 x 14 large format films in terms of resolution for awhile, either.

●Globally popular Nature Aquarium

The first photo book, *Nature Aquarium World Book 1*, was translated into six different languages after its publication in Japan, and it received enthusiastic responses from all over the world. The situation was similar in Japan as well. The

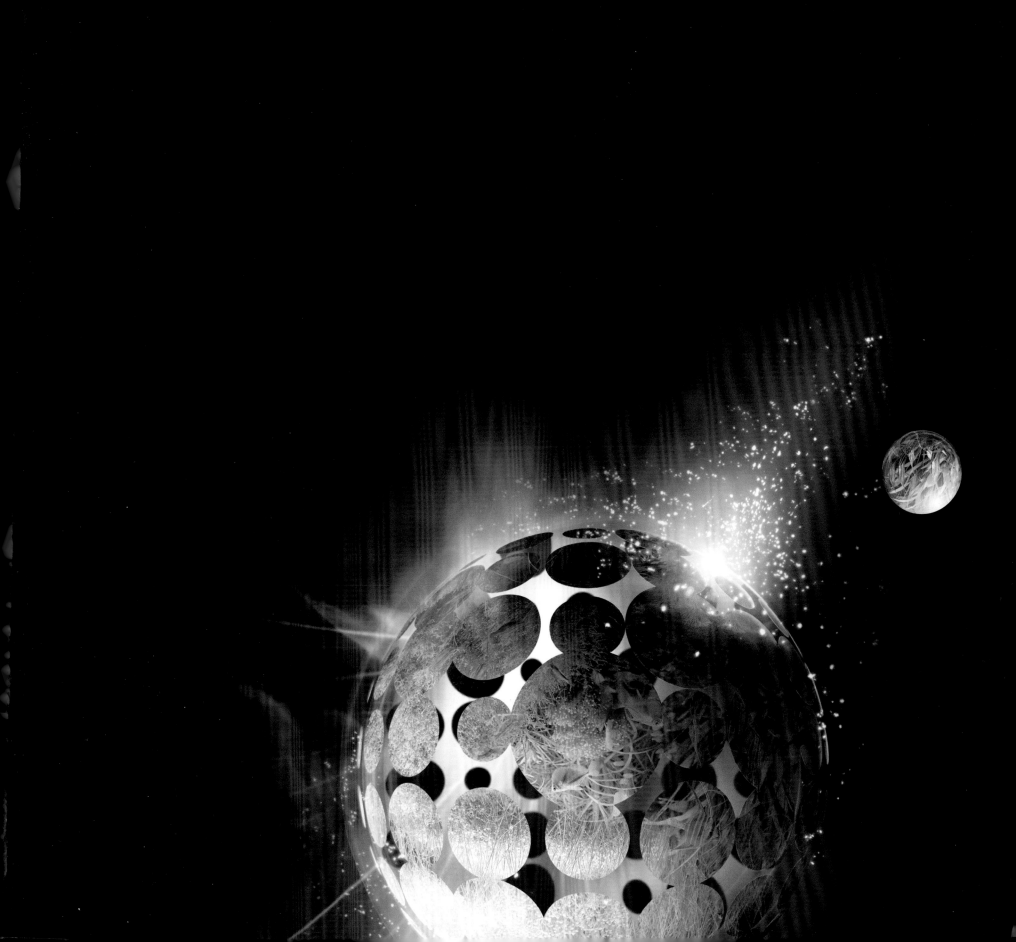

CONTENTS

● The effect of approaching global warming

When we look at things from a broader view, dead trees are becoming more numerous in the mountains. While the problem of dying pine trees has been known for some time, dying oak and beech trees are becoming a serious problem in more recent years. Dead brown oak and beech trees in what should be a solid, green, broadleaf forest is a bizarre sight. The damage is done by certain insect pests that used to live in the southern area, and their range is expanding northward every year. The fact that the amount of snowfall has decreased in the heavy snow belt of Tohoku and Hokuriku areas in recent years and the insect pests can overwinter easily have contributed to the increasing damage. Speaking of global warming, although the decreasing numbers of polar bears and penguins due to the melting glaciers in the North and South Poles along with the rising ocean surface level have often been reported, the damage to familiar plants within Japan has hardly been reported in relation to the global warming until now. Locally, severe rainstorms and larger typhoons have caused frequent floods and landslides in the past few years. The decreasing forests in the mountains and the resulting decrease in their water holding capacity has a lot to do with this, in addition to the effect of global warming. If the water holding capacity of a forest decreases, the surface soil is washed away with rains. A large amount of earth and sand flows into the ocean from the land, and this causes coastal damage, which destroys seaweed. The forest of seaweed nurtures a large amount of living creatures such as fishes and shellfish, and the destruction of the seaweed leads to the collapse of ecosystems in the ocean. The effect of global warming is sneaking up steadily to the familiar nature around us.

● What we can do as a countermeasure against global warming

As newspaper and TV news have been reporting a lot, it is urgent to reduce CO_2 emission to the atmosphere in order to stop the progress of global warming. It is necessary not only to reduce the CO_2 emissions from factories and automobiles but also to increase the green plants that absorb CO_2. I planted trees around my house and company, and I created natural areas that I call Nature Biotope. I believe that more trees should be planted in cities where a large amount of CO_2 is released. This will not only increase the absorption of CO_2 but it might also encourage more people to get interested in nature. If a person could feel the splendor of nature within an arm's reach, that person may realize its importance. All living things, including us humans, inhale oxygen and exhale CO_2. Plants absorb CO_2 and discharge oxygen through photosynthesis. If this relationship were well balanced in the global scale, the problem of global warming would not have occurred. Doesn't realizing this simple fact help us see what we must do now?

● The significance of creating Nature Aquarium

It was difficult initially to get people to understand the significance of adding CO_2, even in Nature Aquarium. People thought that fish would suffer if CO_2 were added to an aquarium. Fish will suffocate if CO_2 is added to a fish-only bare bottom tank or if an excessive amount of CO_2 is added by ignoring the level of photosynthesis of aquatic plants. However, if CO_2 is added to an aquarium that is planted with aquatic plants and it with adequately bright light, it will promote photosynthesis of aquatic plants. The number of people who understood this increased gradually through adding CO_2 in an aquarium and demonstrating aquatic plants performing photosynthesis. Now it is almost a common sense to inject CO_2 in an aquatic plant layout. Aquatic plants grow well by performing photosynthesis in an aquarium, and the oxygen released by aquatic plants supports the lives of fish, shrimp, and microorganisms. This is not different from the mechanism of an ecosystem in nature. CO_2 is talked about as the source of all evils in the global warming issue these days. While excessive CO_2 certainly accelerates the global warming, it is a fact that plants cannot live without CO_2 and animals cannot live without plants. Isn't it important for us to recognize just how much the rich, natural environment absorbed CO_2 and released oxygen in the past? If we had an environment in which plants grew well and the demand and supply of CO_2 was well balanced, global warming would not have become such a huge issue. Although it is important to reduce CO_2, I believe what is really important is to restore nature to a point where ecosystems are maintained. I chose the name "Nature Aquarium" based on two points: it not only reflects the beauty of nature but also has the function of an ecosystem. In Nature Aquarium, we learn from nature and create an environment in which fish can live comfortably. The appearance of fish swimming pleasantly in an aquarium along with beautiful, dense aquatic plants soothes our minds. I hope that becoming conscious of nature through the beauty and fun of keeping such an aquascape can lead to putting a stop to environmental destruction. I hope that this photo book can get more people interested in Nature Aquarium and in turn in nature.

layouts that expressed nature in an aquarium, using limited types of aquatic plants with rocks and driftwood as composition materials, must have looked refreshing to people who were only familiar with aquatic plant layouts that looked like flower gardens. It seems that the Japanese atmosphere that I unconsciously expressed in layouts was thought to relate to Wabi-sabi of Zen Buddhism and Japanese tea ceremony, which have attracted attention overseas. Therefore, Nature Aquarium was called Zen Aquarium in some countries. Yamato Numa Ebi (*Caridina japonica*) that I used to control algae in aquariums became known as "Amano Shrimp." As these new terms would indicate, the book seems to have had some effects on the overall aquarium hobby in the world. The increasing popularity of Nature Aquarium in the world is evident through the number of entries that are submitted to ADA's International Aquatic Plant Layout Contest, a number that has been increasing every year. In 2009, we received 1,342 entries from 51 countries around the world. The majority of these layouts were produced using the Nature Aquarium layout method. This seems to indicate that a universal image of nature, rather than the Japanese atmosphere of Nature Aquarium, appeals to people. Being able to enjoy the image of nature by keeping it close by might be the reason why Nature Aquarium has become popular in the world. Human beings seem to have an inherent sensitivity that compels us to keep things that make us feel closer to nature, such as plants and animals. I realized this when I visited the Amazon looking for the native habitats of tropical fish and aquatic plants in order to take their photographs. I was quite

amazed to find that native indigenous people were growing ornamental plants and keeping birds and animals as pets in their houses, something unexpected in a village surrounded by a dense jungle. Our desire to keep animals and plants nearby must be a human instinct. The soft colors and shimmering lights of Nature Aquarium are said to relax and soothe people's minds. A small ecosystem thriving in an aquarium enables us to see the activities of nature. In today's world where once familiar nature is disappearing around us, Nature Aquarium may take the place of nature and bring us peace of mind. The fact that Nature Aquarium is enjoyed all over the world and that nature is disappearing around us may just be two sides of the same coin.

● **Rapidly disappearing nature around us**

The oldest layout in this book was created in 1985 and the newest one was created in 2009. Unfortunately there wasn't any existing film for any layouts that were created before 1985. The length of time over which these photographs were taken, counting only those for which film still exists, stretches over a quarter of a century. It makes me somewhat sentimental to think of that. I reviewed all the layouts chronologically as I compiled the materials for this photo book. Old layouts reminded me of the times. They also made me realize that not only my life has changed but also the environment around us has greatly changed as well. The once familiar environment has disappeared rapidly from around us in the past quarter of a century. The basic principle of Nature Aquarium is to learn from nature. I may be reacting very sensitively to the subtle changes in nature around us because I have been creating Nature

Aquarium layouts.

My home and my company are located in the suburbs of Niigata city. Both places are surrounded by rustic scenery. Normally, the idea of rustic scenery may conjure up an image of a rich, green environment alive with living creatures such as frogs, snakes, spiders and insects. However, in actuality such living creatures have practically disappeared. Leopard frogs that I often saw in my childhood disappeared about 20 years ago. People around me, including farmers, did not notice this until I pointed it out. Tree frogs used to sing loudly at night everywhere, but the number of adult tree frogs that overwinter has declined drastically. Nowadays, we can only find a few small ones that are born each year. In an ecological food chain, insects are eaten by frogs, which are in turn eaten by snakes. If a frog is not found in an environment, it means that the ecosystem in that environment is collapsing. The causes include not only changes in the farming environment that were brought about by efficiency improvements, but they also include global level environmental changes. When it comes to recreating natural scenery in a small space, it makes no difference to me whether it's an aquarium or the company premises. I planted approximately three hundred trees around my company building. These trees grew densely and now the building looks like it was built in a forest. The forest has not been tended except for weeding, which is done a few times a year. Trees still grew much taller than the building. Snakes, Japanese raccoon dogs, and various birds showed up from somewhere and are now living in the forest. A small ecosystem is thriving in the forest.

TAKASHI AMANO
NATURE AQUARIUM
COMPLETE WORKS
1985-1991

DATA

		Aquatic Plants			
Date	October, 1985		*Rotala macrandra*	*Echinodorus major*	*Nannostomus trifasciatus*
Aquarium	W71 x D39 x H32 (in)		*Rotala rotundifolia*	*Echinodorus latifolius*	*Thoracocharax stellatus*
Lighting	40W x 8 units, turned on for 10 hours		*Ceratapteris thalictroides*	*Echinodorus bleheri*	*Hyphessobrycon sweglesi*
Filter	External Filter x 2 units, Bio Rio		*Hygrophila lacustrus*	*Cryptocoryne balansae*	*Nematobrycon palmeri*
Substrate	Oisosuna (Sea gravel), Power Sand		*Eichhornia azurea*	*Nymphaea lotus*	*Hemigrammus bleheri*
CO₂	2 bubbles per second		*Alternanthera reineckii*	*Crinum natans forma crispus*	*Paracheirodon axelrodi*
Additives	Brighty K		*Fontinalis antipyretica*	*Crinum calamistratum*	*Otocinclus* sp.
Water Change	1/3 once a week		*Microsorum pteropus*	Animals / *Pterophyllum altum*	*Caridina japonica*
Water Quality	Temperature 79°F; pH 6.8; TH 20mg/l		*Vallisneria spiralis*	*Hyphessobrycon megalopterus*	

The Balance of Nature

This is a layout that I created about twenty five years ago. It is one of the oldest for which some photographs are still remaining. It was made into an extra large poster titled "The Balance of Nature", and the five thousand prints that were produced at that time sold out in no time. This aquascape was maintained in a beautiful condition for as long as five years. Besides the fact that it is a lot of work to redo a large aquarium, by the time Nature Aquarium was established, it was already quite normal to maintain a finished layout for two to three years. Being somewhat of a slacker by nature, I'm not good at keeping up with daily chores. Just looking at stem plants to see if they have enough potassium or just the thought of having to trim them soon is a drag. Therefore, for a layout that is intended to be maintained for a long time, I developed some ways to make sure that it can be maintained in good condition without being really high maintenance. For example, I use ferns and *Cryptocoryne* primarily instead of aquatic plants that require frequent trimmings, such as stem plants. I may use some techniques that allow various aquatic plants in an aquarium to wax and wane naturally, and as a result, an aquascape often ends up having a rather different impression in a year. Long term maintenance is one of the most important concepts of Nature Aquarium. The style in which aquatic plants are allowed to grow and produce an aquascape naturally relates well to the basic principles of Nature Aquarium. Maintaining an aquascape in good condition is the same as having a good balance in the ecosystem inside an aquarium. Algae hardly develop and fish seldom get sick in such an environment. A new life is born through natural breeding and the next generation of fish appears in an aquarium that has been maintained for a long time. Nature in a glass box tells us that ecosystem remains in a good shape for a long period of time in a well-balanced environment.

Flower Garden Style vs. Natural Style

Previously in Japan, aquatic plant layouts were divided largely into Dutch style (Dutch Aquarium) and Japanese style. The Dutch style is the method that combines groups of aquatic plants in a geometric manner to enjoy colorful, collective beauty of aquatic plants. On the other hand, the Japanese style recreates elements that exist in nature inside an aquarium, doing so by using natural materials, such as rocks and driftwood, in addition to aquatic plants. I find this method of differentiation somewhat questionable. If anything, it is more appropriate to call the Dutch style a "flower garden style" and the Japanese style a "natural style," based on my own interpretation. I named my aquatic plant layout Nature Aquarium in the sense that it is a "natural style".

While both the Japanese and Dutch styles seem to perceive an aquatic plant layout as a type of scenery, they differ greatly in the way they maintain a layout. Dutch Aquarium requires a lot of effort to maintain it because a layout is maintained by cutting and replanting the tops of stem plants. In Nature Aquarium, maintenance is easier since the layout is maintained by trimming plants. Although the flower garden style of layout was the mainstream in the world in the past, Nature Aquarium is widely recognized in the world now and is gaining many followers.

When I review contest entries, I find that Asian hobbyists are more skilled at recreating natural sceneries. However, Europeans seem better at recreating the habitats of living creatures. Germans in particular have very different ideas from the Japanese about natural environments. While both Japan and Germany prospered through manufacturing, Germany seems to be much better at making things that are used for an extended period of time. Although Japan achieved economic recovery and the status of a great economic power after the WWII, the country developed at the expense of nature. It is just a façade, like an empty house of cards.

When a German visitor came to ADA, I explained to him that a lot of Japanese consider us a strange company because of being located in woods. He told me in a matter-of-fact way that it is pretty normal in Germany. Germans and Japanese have a very different attitude toward environment. Japanese sometimes ask why we planted dwarf bamboo around trees instead of installing a lawn. The reason for this is that bamboo offers shade and a place to hide for small creatures, such as frogs, snakes, and insects. A majority of the buildings in Japan have been built primarily for people. I hope that the wooded area around my company stays as a paradise for living creatures. About 60% of the company's premises are a wooded area and more than half of the company construction cost was spent on it. People thought that I was an oddball for taking out a loan to plant trees at that time, but I went all out and even got electric wires installed underground. This was done so that the trees do not interfere with wires as they grow, and also to avoid cutting trees down if electrical wires were to be installed underground in the future. I often work feverishly, pressed for time. I find it rather comforting to see the trees swaying gently in the wind when I happen to look outside the window. Working in the environment surrounded by greenery may have something in common with Nature Aquarium concept of nurturing living things in amongst plants.

DATA

Date	December, 1985	*Cryptocoryne costata*
Aquarium	W47 x D39 x H29.5 (in)	*Cryptocoryne wendtii* (**brown**)
Lighting	20W x 10 units, turned on for 10 hours	*Crinum natans forma crispus*
Filter	External Filter x 2 units, Bio Rio	*Crinum calamistratum*
Substrate	Kaisan suna (Sea sand), Power Sand	*Echinodorus tenellus*
CO₂	2 bubbles per second	Animals *Pelvicachromis taeniatus*
Water Change	1/3 once every two weeks	*Pelvicachromis subocellatus*
Water Quality	Temperature 82°F; pH 6.9; TH 50mg/l	*Pelvicachromis humilis*
Aquatic Plants	*Anubias barteri* var. *barteri*	*Pelvicachromis roloffi*
	Anubias heterophylla	*Nanochromis dimidiatus*
	Anubias afzelii	*Nanochromis nudiceps*
	Anubias congensis	*Nanochromis parilus*
	Anubias auriculata	*Nanochromis transvestitus*
	Anubias barteri var. *nana*	*Otocinclus* sp.
	Bolbitis heudelotii	*Caridina japonica*
	Fontinalis antipyretica	

The Origin of Nature Aquarium

Yoroigata was a place where aquatic plants grew densely and myriad ecosystems thrived. It was a lagoon that existed near the house that I grew up in during the late 1950s. It was a place that looked like the village from the time depicted in the Japanese animation film "My Neighbor Totoro." Kids at that time helped out around the house a lot. They caught fish and collected lotus root and water chestnuts for fun. We played in Yoroigata everyday when we came home from school. Nature was a part of our daily life. I was able to see a school of small fish swimming between aquatic plants. A glimpse of their silver scales used to give me such an excitement. Being the leader of the pack, I used to take younger kids to catch fish in the lagoon. While we split the catch evenly, I usually claimed smaller pretty fishes, such as Japanese bitterling and *Rhinogobius* (freshwater goby), and let the others take large, edible ones like carp and catfish. I carried my small fish in a shoe and walked home over a mile under the scorching sun. By the time I got home, the fish were all dead from the heat and the lack of oxygen. My grandmother scolded me every time saying "What good does it do to bring such little things?" One day I took some fish home again in a shoe along with some aquatic plants, and to my amazement, not a fish died. I realized then that aquatic plants are essential to fish. I believe that this experience strengthened my special interest in aquatic plants. As young as I was, I had a vague understanding that aquatic plants kept water clean and fish do not live where there are no aquatic plants. I learned right there in nature that living things in the waterfront gathered around the aquatic plants and formed an ecosystem together. The underwater scene at Yoroigata in my childhood is still vivid in my mind as the miniature model of an ecosystem. Looking back, I see that these experiences became the origin of Nature Aquarium.

DATA

Date	January, 1990
Aquarium	W71 x D63 x H35 (in)
Lighting	40W x 9 units, turned on for 10 hours
Filter	Original External Filter, Bio Rio
Substrate	Akadama Ceramic, Power Sand
CO₂	2 bubbles per second
Additives	Brighty K
Water Change	1/3 once a week
Water Quality	Temperature 79°F; pH 6.8; TH 20mg/l
Aquatic Plants	*Alternanthera reineckii*
	Rotala macrandra
	Rotala rotundifolia
	Echinodorus horemanii Green
	Echinodorus horemanii Red
	Echinodorus bleheri
	Echinodorus latifolius
	Echinodorus tenellus

Echinodorus aschersonianus
Lagenandra ovata
Echinodorus horizontalis
Cryptocoryne wendtii (brown)
Anubias barteri var. barteri
Anubias barteri var. nana
Anubias congensis
Anubias gracilis
Anubias lanceolata
Crinum natans forma crispus
Crinum calamistratum
Microsorum pteropus
Bolbitis heudelotii

Animals / *Pterophyllum altum*
Hemigrammus bleheri
Otocinclus sp.
Caridina japonica

DATA

Date /June, 1991
Aquarium /W71 x D24 x H24 (in)
Lighting /40W x 6 units, turned on for 10 hours
Filter /Original External Filter, Bio Rio
Substrate /Oisosuna (Sea gravel), Power Sand
CO₂ /2 bubbles per second
Additives /Brighty K
Water Change /1/2 once a week
Water Quality /Temperature 75°F; pH 6.8; TH 20mg/l

Aquatic Plants /*Riccia fluitans*
                Eleocharis acicularis
Animals /*Pungtungia herzir*

Using *Riccia* in a Layout

Riccia has been used in aquariums for a relatively long time. However, its use was not originally for a layout. Although a majority of the people think of a beautiful, green carpet grown densely over the substrate when they hear the name *Riccia* nowadays, this was not the case until 20 years ago. Until that time, there were not many people using *Riccia* in such a manner except for a few enthusiasts. Back then *Riccia* was grown on the water surface for herbivore fish to graze on, or as a nesting site for gouramis, or as a

hiding place for guppies or other fish fry. *Riccia* on the water surface grows rapidly with adequate light.

Riccia grows naturally in many parts of the world. The majority of *Riccia* floats on the water surface, bunched up at waterfronts of slow running rivers and ponds. When the water level drops, it grows by hanging onto damp soil, but it does not attach itself to driftwood or a rock as Willow Moss does. Consequently, it was considered unsuitable for use in an aquatic plant layout for many years. However, I have also known *Riccia* to grow submerged in nearby rice paddies. Therefore, I often wondered about using *Riccia* in a layout by taking advantage of this characteristic.

So I initially tried the method of wrapping Riccia on a rock with a nylon thread. I considered wrapping *Riccia* on a thin, flat stone and covering the substrate with the *Riccia* clad stones. I finally succeeded in growing a dense carpet of the floating liverwort *Riccia* through numerous trials and errors. The sight of *Riccia* adorned with beautiful, pearl-like air bubbles caught many people's attention. I also developed Riccia Line in the same color as *Riccia* to make it inconspicuous in a layout and a thin, rectangular Riccia Stone, which is easy to wrap *Riccia* on. They caught on at once as a method that anybody could use in order to use *Riccia* easily in a layout.

Art is unexpectedly commonplace around us. *Riccia*, which was once regarded as a weed in a rice paddy, became an indispensible, attractive plant when it comes to an aquatic plant layout.

AMANO Style Layout

I personally do not like a very intricate layout with such attention to minute details since it seems too constricting. On the contrary, I often find a layout that appears to be nonchalantly put together more appealing, although "nonchalantly" may not be the right word for it. When it comes to my own layout, I like a hassle-free aquarium in which aquatic plants are allowed to grow naturally and create their own scenery. It may sound lazy, but it is actually the secret for enjoying Nature Aquarium for a long time. A layout that is crafted with overly great finesse is tiring to look at, and it is also difficult to maintain over a long period of time. It is without doubt too constricting to keep up for a long time. The same thing is true for a large aquarium set up in a public place. It is important to provide an unpretentious, casual atmosphere of water and greenery. The very atmosphere creates the harmony between the surrounding space and the aquarium. Additionally, I start a layout by choosing materials first. I look at available layout materials and decide how to make the most of the materials based on the ambiance of the installation site. This extemporaneous factor helps to create the atmosphere that is appropriate for the site. Creating a layout at one stretch builds the momentum naturally. This is only possible with long experience. I agonized over the placement of a rock for many hours until I finally reached this level of accomplishment. There are an infinite number of patterns for rock arrangement. The key is to find the ultimate position for a rock out of the infinite choices as quickly as possible. I used to struggle with the placement of rocks until two or three in the morning. I finally settled on the best arrangement and went to bed. When I woke up the next morning and looked at the rocks, I would get totally disappointed and would redo the arrangement all over again. It went on like this for a long time. As a result, I can make a satisfactory rock arrangement in a matter of minutes now. No matter how large an aquarium, a few tens of minutes would be sufficient. The sense of force is important in a rock arrangement. The sense of force cannot be produced no matter how long you spend agonizing over it. The same thing is true with driftwood and aquatic plant arrangements. Dwelling on an arrangement does not produce an unpretentious, natural looking layout. What it boils down to is how much you have observed nature. After all, Nature Aquarium is not built in a day.

DATA

Date	October, 1991	Cryptocoryne pontederifolia
Aquarium	W71 x D39 x H31.5 (in)	Echinodorus horemanii
Lighting	40W x 10 units, turned on for 10 hours	Crinum natans forma crispus
Filter	Original External Filter x 2 units, Bio Rio	Crinum calamistratum
Substrate	Oisosuna (Sea gravel), Power Sand	Fontinalis antipyretica
CO₂	2 bubbles per second	Echinodorus tenellus
Additives	Brighty K	Animals / Phenacogrammus interruptus
Water Change	1/3 once every two weeks	Bathyaethiops caudomaculatus
Water Quality	Temperature 79°F; pH 6.9; TH 20mg/l	Paracheirodon simulans
Aquatic Plants	Cryptocoryne retrospiralis	Iguanodectes spilurus
	Cryptocoryne wendtii (green)	Otocinclus sp.
	Cryptocoryne wendtii (brown)	Caridina japonica
	Cryptocoryne costata	

DATA

Date	December, 1991
Aquarium	W71 x D24 x H24 (in)
Lighting	40W x 6 units, turned on for 10 hours
Filter	Original External Filter, Bio Rio
Substrate	Oisosuna (Sea gravel), Power Sand
CO₂	2 bubbles per second
Additives	Brighty K
Water Change	1/2 once a week
Water Quality	Temperature 81°F; pH 6.9; TH 20mg/l

Aquatic Plants / *Glossostigma elatinoides*

Animals / *Paracheirodon simulans*
Otocinclus sp.
Caridina japonica
Neocaridina sp.

Secret Story of *Glossostigma*

Although *Glossostigma* is now an old standby for aquatic plant layouts, it was quite a rare plant at one time and only a few enthusiasts grew it in small amounts. About twenty years ago, I wanted to create a layout with this aquatic plant more than anything and had a vendor ship every one of them that they could find in Europe. Unfortunately the shipment was held up in customs because the plant had never been imported into Japan, and no one knew what family it belonged to. Just about all of them melted in the summer heat. I was taking underwater photographs in the ocean near Sado Island at that time. When I heard the news by phone from my staff, I thought that my attempt was a complete failure. However, I set down determinedly to revive the plants from the sad condition they were in.

I put a few remaining leaves of *Glossostigma* in an aquarium and tried all sorts of things, but not a single sprout developed for two months. Then, apparently something worked one day, and it suddenly started growing. Throwing driftwood into the water, turning the water soft accidentally, or adding some nutrients that contained iron and organic acids might have had something to do with it. Eventually, a simple layout was produced solely with the *Glossostigma*, and it created a great sensation in the aquarium industry. One can turn a misfortune into a profit, because giving up means curtains for your endeavor. The plant taught me a great lesson.

TAKASHI AMANO
NATURE AQUARIUM
COMPLETE WORKS

1992-1993

DATA

Date	/May, 1992	*Eusteralis verticillata*
Aquarium	/W47 x D18 x H18 (in)	*Rotala rotundifolia*
Lighting	/20W x 10 units, turned on for 10 hours	*Rotala macrandra*
Filter	/External Filter, Bio Rio	*Potamogeton mascarensis*
Substrate	/Oisosuna (Sea gravel), Power Sand	*Alternanthera reineckii*
CO₂	/Pollen Glass Beetle 50, 5 bubbles per second via CO₂	*Ludwigia inclinata*
	Beetle Counter	*Cabomba australis*
Additives	/Brighty K; Green Brighty STEP 2; Green Gain	*Bacopa monnieri*
Water Change	/1/2 once a week	*Hygrophila corymbosa*
Water Quality	/Temperature 81°F; pH 6.9; TH 50mg/l	*Echinodorus horemanii*
Aquatic Plants	/*Echinodorus tenellus*	*Isoetes japonica*
	Eleocharis acicularis	Animals/*Paracheirodon axelrodi*
	Anubias barteri var. *nana*	*Hemigrammus bleheri*
	Cryptocoryne costata	*Nematobrycon palmeri*
	Cryptocoryne balansae	*Caridina japonica*
	Bolbitis heudelotii	*Otocinclus* sp.
	Hemianthus micranthemoides	

DATA

Date	January, 1992
Aquarium	W47 x D18 x H18 (in)
Lighting	20W x 8 units, turned on for 10 hours
Filter	External Filter, Bio Rio
Substrate	Yaki akadama, Power Sand
CO₂	3 bubbles per second by CO₂ Pollen Glass
Additives	Brighty K
Water Change	1/2 once a week
Water Quality	Temperature 75°F; pH 6.9; TH 50mg/l
Aquatic Plants	*Riccia fluitans*
	Eleocharis acicularis
	Sagittaria sp.
	Cabomba acquatica
	Limnophila sessiliflora
	Ceratophyllum demersum
	Bacopa rotundifolia
	Ludwigia ovalis
	Eusteralis verticillata
Animals	*Oryzias latipes*
	Caridina japonica

DATA
Date   /May, 1992
Aquarium   /W18 x D12 x H12 (in)
Lighting   /27W x 3 units, turned on for 11 hours
Filter   /External Filter, Bio Rio
Substrate   /Oisosuna (Sea gravel), Power Sand
CO₂   /Pollen Glass, 1 bubble per second via CO₂
             Bubble Counter
Additives   /Green Brighty STEP 2
Water Change /1/3 once every five days
Water Quality /Temperature 77°F; pH 6.9; TH 20mg/l
Aquatic Plants /*Glossostigma elatinoides*
             Eleocharis acicularis
             Riccia fluitans
             Potamogeton gayi
Animals   /*Pseudomugil furcatus*
             Caridina japonica
             Otocinclus sp.

DATA
Date   /April, 1992
Aquarium   /W18 x D12 x H12 (in)
Lighting   /27W x 3 units, turned on for 12hours
Filter   /External Filter, Bio Rio
Substrate   /Oisosuna (Sea gravel), Power Sand
CO₂   /Pollen Glass, 1 bubble per second via CO₂
             Bubble Counter
Additives   /Green Brighty STEP 2
Water Change /1/3 once a week
Water Quality /Temperature 79°F; pH 6.8; TH 20mg/l
Aquatic Plants /*Riccia fluitans*
             Mayaca fluviatilis
             Cabomba australis
             Microsorum pteropus
             Didiplis diandra
             Rotala macrandra
             Rotala wallichii
             Limnophila aquatica
Animals   /*Hemigrammus pulcher*
             Caridina japonica
             Otocinclus sp.

DATA

Date	June, 1992	Aquatic Plants	*Glossostigma elatinoides*
Aquarium	W22 x D22 x H22 (in)		*Eleocharis acicularis*
Lighting	Halogen Lamp 150W x 1 unit, turned on for 12 hours		*Fontinalis antipyretica*
Filter	External Filter, Bio Rio, Bamboo Charcoal		*Aponogeton madagascariensis*
Substrate	Oisosuna (Sea gravel), Power Sand		*Cryptocoryne balansae*
CO₂	Pollen Glass Beetle 40, 3 bubbles per second via CO₂ Beetle Counter	Animals	*Paracheirodon axelrodi*
Additives	Brighty K; Green Brighty STEP 3		*Caridina japonica*
Water Change	1/3 once a week		*Otocinclus* sp.
Water Quality	Temperature 77°F; pH 6.2; TH 20mg/l		

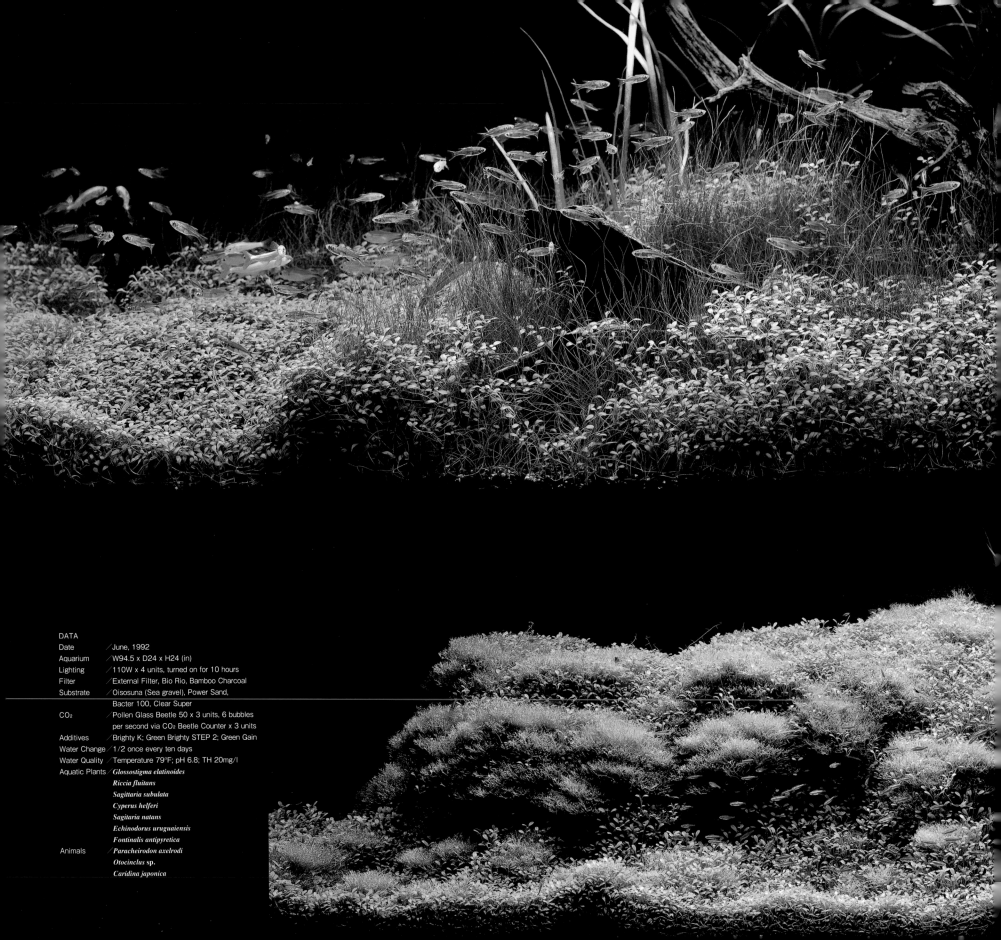

DATA
Date ╱ June, 1992
Aquarium ╱ W94.5 x D24 x H24 (in)
Lighting ╱ 110W x 4 units, turned on for 10 hours
Filter ╱ External Filter, Bio Rio, Bamboo Charcoal
Substrate ╱ Oisosuna (Sea gravel), Power Sand,
Bacter 100, Clear Super
CO₂ ╱ Pollen Glass Beetle 50 x 3 units, 6 bubbles
per second via CO₂ Beetle Counter x 3 units
Additives ╱ Brighty K; Green Brighty STEP 2; Green Gain
Water Change ╱ 1/2 once every ten days
Water Quality ╱ Temperature 79°F; pH 6.8; TH 20mg/l
Aquatic Plants ╱ *Glossostigma elatinoides*
Riccia fluitans
Sagittaria subulata
Cyperus helferi
Sagitaria natans
Echinodorus uruguaiensis
Fontinalis antipyretica
Animals ╱ *Paracheirodon axelrodi*
Otocinclus sp.
Caridina japonica

DATA

Date	June, 1992
Aquarium	W71 x D24 x H24 (in)
Lighting	20W x 24 units, turned on for 10 hours
Filter	External Filter, Bio Rio, Bamboo Charcoal
Substrate	Oisosuna (Sea gravel), Power Sand, Bacter 100, Clear Super, Iron Bottom
CO₂	Pollen Glass Beetle 50 x 2 units, 5 bubbles per second via CO₂ Beetle Counter x 2 units
Additives	Brighty K; Green Brighty STEP 3; Green Gain
Water Change	1/2 once a week
Water Quality	Temperature 77°F; pH 7.0; TH 20mg/l
Aquatic Plants	*Glossostigma elatinoides*
	Eleocharis acicularis
	Vallisneria spiralis
Animals	*Telmatherina ladigesi*
	Hemigrammopetersius caudalis
	Plecoglossus altivelis
	Otocinclus sp.
	Caridina japonica

DATA

Date	／July, 1992
Aquarium	／W71 x D63 x H35 (in)
Lighting	／40W x 15 units, turned on for 12 hours
Filter	／External Filter, Bio Rio, Bamboo Charcoal
Substrate	／Oisosuna (Sea gravel), Power Sand, Bacter 100, Clear Super
CO₂	／Pollen Glass Beetle 50 x 4 units, 7 bubbles per second via CO₂ Beetle Counter x 4 units
Additives	／Brighty K; Green Brighty STEP 3; Green Gain
Water Change	／1/2 once a week

Water Quality ／Temperature 81°F; pH 7.0; TH 20mg/l

Aquatic Plants ／*Glossostigma elatinoides*
Eleocharis acicularis
Microsorum pteropus
Cryptocoryne balansae
Echinodorus horemanii
Crinum natans forma crispus
Crinum calamistratum
Cryptocoryne retrospiralis

Animals ／*Symphysodon aequifasciatus* var.
Hemigrammus bleheri
Caridina japonica
Otocinclus sp.

The Most Memorable Turquoise Discus

Discus are the most famous fish, along with angelfish, in the family of cichlids native to the Amazon. The characteristically disc-shaped body and unique patterns covering the body surface are the major appeals of this fish. It is the king of the fishes that many of us wish to keep in an aquatic layout at least once. However, it is only in a large aquarium with adequate depth and water volume where the real appeal of this fish can be brought out. Discus requires a large swimming space and a large volume of food, which tends to foul the water, thus requiring the high enough water volume to support them. A simple layout with large aquatic plants is suitable for keeping this fish, rather than a layout with a complex design and a lot of stem plants. The charm of discus can be brought out fully by allowing them to swim freely in a relaxed manner.

Although I still occasionally wish to put discus in a layout, I have unfortunately not been able to find a worthy fish for some time. It may be because of the magnificent quality of the turquoise discus in this aquascape. Its well-balanced body shape and beautiful turquoise color were simply majestic. This aquascape with the turquoise discus has been the most memorable one to me.

DATA

Date	╱October, 1992	Aquatic Plants╱	*Riccia fluitans*
Aquarium	╱W71 x D63 x H35 (in)		*Eleocharis acicularis*
Lighting	╱20W x 24 units, turned on for 10 hours		*Sagittaria subulata*
Filter	╱External Filter, Bio Rio, Bamboo Charcoal		*Sagittaria graminea* var. *platyphylla*
Substrate	╱Oisosuna (Sea gravel), Power Sand, Bacter 100		*Anubias barteri* var. *nana*
CO₂	╱Pollen Glass Beetle 50 x 2 units, 5 bubbles per		*Anubias barteri* var. *barteri*
	second via CO₂ Beetle Counter x 2 units	Animals╱	*Pterophyllum altum*
Additives	╱Brighty K; Green Brighty STEP 3		*Hyphessobrycon sweglesi*
Water Change	╱1/2 once every two weeks		*Caridina japonica*
Water Quality	╱Temperature 79°F; pH 7.0; TH 20mg/l		*Otocinclus* sp.

To Place an Aquarium in a Living Room

While I have developed various pieces of aquarium equipment, every one of them has been something that I wanted personally. Although I developed the equipment out of necessity for growing aquatic plants, it started out with the desire to "make the aquarium more attractive." At that time in Japan, an aquarium was generally considered a "container to keep fish" and often delegated to the top of a shoe closet in a foyer or in a corner of a hallway. The idea of having it as a part of the decor of the living room was not even a consideration. It seemed to me that the poor design of an aquarium and its equipment was the reason for this treatment. So

for an aquarium to gain citizenship in a household, I thought it was essential to provide an aquarium and equipment elegant enough to be part of the decor of a living room.

Easy to use equipment naturally has a good design and shape. It is not the aesthetics that is given the priority, but instead the appearance becomes refined naturally while working on a design optimizing the ease of use. Good, easy to use equipment, whether it is a car, a camera or a watch, often has a good design and shape. This idea is the origin of Nature Aquarium Goods.

The ideas for product development sprung out like a fountain. All the knowledge and experience about aquariums that I cultivated

over the years came in handy. The detailed records that I kept in a notebook proved very useful as well. I even finished an entire concept for a new product in one day. Glass became the standard material so that the equipment can disappear into an aquascape unobtrusively, as well as to pursue the simple beauty of an aquarium. It also offered the warmth of an object hand-crafted by a craftsman. I believe that the insistence on good craftsmanship brought pleasing consequences, such as an attachment to a good tool and the satisfaction of using the tool.

DATA

		Aquatic Plants	*Glossostigma elatinoides*		*Rotala macrandra*
Date	December, 1992		*Eleocharis acicularis*		*Aleternanthera reineckii forma lilacina*
Aquarium	W71 x D24 x H24 (in)		*Riccia fluitans*		*Hygrophila lacustrus*
Lighting	20W x 24 units, turned on for 10 hours		*Litricularia gibba* sp.	Animals /	*Hyphessobrycon sweglesi*
Filter	External Filter, Bio Rio, Bamboo Charcoal		*Isoetes japonica*		*Caridina japonica*
Substrate	Oisosuna (Sea gravel), Power Sand, Bacter 100,		*Sagittaria graminea* var. *platyphylla*		*Otocinclus* sp.
	Clear Super, Iron Bottom		*Eusteralis yatabeana*		
CO₂	Pollen Glass Beetle 50 x 2 units, 6 bubbles per		*Eusteralis stellata*		
	second via CO₂ Beetle Counter x 2 units		*Rotala wallichii*		
Additives	Brighty K; Green Brighty STEP 3; Green Gain		*Rotala rotundifolia*		
Water Change	1/2 once a week		*Eusteralis verticillata*		
Water Quality	Temperature 79°F; pH 7.0; TH 50mg/l				

Four corners as the key point of a layout

When I explain the important points for creating a layout in a seminar, I often advise people to put an effort into the four corners of a layout. This is because a lot of people tend to overlook the four corners, although everyone works hard to produce the center of a layout.

The four corners are important for taking a landscape picture as well. The large format camera that I use shows an image upside down, and on top of that, the four corners of the image appear dim and are hard to see. Therefore, I developed a habit of looking at four corners closely. I also make painstakingly sure that the image is in focus, especially when the image is upside down. I move the camera if a single weed is in the way. Some people may think that a photo taken with large format film is supposed to be trimmed. However, I do not trim my pictures for the very reason that they are taken with large format film. It is a shame to waste the ability of the camera to delineate the details.

There are other benefits of skills developed through photography for examining a layout. When setting a camera exposure, I look at a landscape by converting it into a monochromatic image in my mind. This is to find the area that reflects light equivalent to 18% gray. The proper exposure can be set easily by looking for an area with a reflection rate around 18% gray, which is a standard for exposure meters, and measuring the reflection with an exposure meter. The sensitivity for colors is cultivated through this practice, which helps when determining the balance of colors of a layout. Dark red appears dark gray in a monochromatic picture, and bright green turns into bright gray that is close to white. In other words, dark red produces a heavy impression, while bright green produces a light impression. Adjusting the balance of a composition by taking the impressions of the colors of aquatic plants into consideration is important for determining the overall impression of a layout.

DATA

Date	╱December, 1992
Aquarium	╱W35 x D18 x H24 (in)
Lighting	╱30W x 4 units, turned on for 9 hours
Filter	╱External Filter, Bio Rio, Bamboo Charcoal
Substrate	╱Kaisansuna (Sea sand)
CO₂	╱Pollen Glass Beetle 30, 3 bubbles per second via CO$_2$ Beetle Counter
Additives	╱Brighty K; Green Gain
Water Change	╱1/2 once a week
Water Quality	╱Temperature 77°F; pH 7.0; TH 20mg/l

Aquatic Plants	╱*Riccia fluitans*
	Fontinalis antipyretica
	Microsorum pteropus
Animals	╱*Hemigrammus bleheri*
	Caridina japonica
	Otocinclus sp.

DATA

Date	╱March, 1993	Aquatic Plants╱*Echinodorus tenellus*	*Eusteralis verticillata*
Aquarium	╱W29.5 x D18 x H18 (in)	*Riccia fluitans*	Animals╱*Hyphessobrycon sweglesi*
Lighting	╱20W x 6 units, turned on for 9 hours	*Fontinalis antipyretica*	*Thoracocharax stellatus*
Filter	╱External Filter, Bio Rio, Bamboo Charcoal	*Echinodorus latifolius*	*Paracheirodon innesi*
Substrate	╱Oisosuna (Sea gravel), Power Sand , Bacter 100,	*Microsorum pteropus*	*Caridina japonica*
	Clear Super, Iron Bottom	*Lagarosiphon madagascariensis*	*Otocinclus* sp.
CO₂	╱Pollen Glass Beetle 40 x 2 units, 3 bubbles per	*Cryptocoryne balansae*	
	second via CO₂ Beetle Counter x 2 units	*Rotala nanjean*	
Additives	╱Brighty K; Green Brighty STEP 3; Green Gain	*Micranthemum unbrosum*	
Water Change	╱1/2 once a week	*Rotala macrandra* sp.	
Water Quality	╱Temperature 77°F; pH 6.9; TH 50mg/l	*Eusteralis stellata*	

DATA

Date　　　　／April, 1993
Aquarium　　／W94.5 x D24 x H24 (in)
Lighting　　 ／110W x 4 units, turned on for 10 hours
Filter　　　　／External Filter, Bio Rio, Bamboo Charcoal
Substrate　　／Oisosuna (Sea gravel), Power Sand, Bacter 100,
　　　　　　　Clear Super
CO₂　　　　　／Pollen Glass Beetle 50 x 3 units, 5 bubbles per
　　　　　　　second via CO₂ Beetle Counter x 3 units
Additives　　／Brighty K; Green Brighty STEP 3; Green Gain
Water Change／1/2 once a week
Water Quality／Temperature 79°F; pH 6.8; TH 20mg/l
Aquatic Plants／*Glossostigma elatinoides*
　　　　　　　Eleocharis acicularis
　　　　　　　Riccia fluitans
Animals　　　／*Paracheirodon simulans*
　　　　　　　Caridina japonica
　　　　　　　Otocinclus sp.

DATA

Date	May, 1993	Water Quality	Temperature 79°F; pH 7.0; TH 20mg/l
Aquarium	W47 x D39 x H29.5 (in)	Aquatic Plants	*Eleocharis acicularis*
Lighting	20W x 20 units, turned on for 10 hours		*Microsorum pteropus*
Filter	External Filter, Bio Rio, Bamboo Charcoal		*Fontinalis antipyretica*
Substrate	Oisosuna (Sea gravel), Power Sand, Bacter 100,		*Cryptocoryne balansae*
	Clear Super	Animals	*Nematobrycon palmeri*
CO₂	Pollen Glass Beetle 50, 5 bubbles per second		*Hemigrammus bleheri*
	via CO₂ Beetle Counter		*Moenkhausia pittieri*
Additives	Brighty K; Green Brighty STEP 3; Green Gain		*Caridina japonica*
Water Change	1/2 once a week		*Otocinclus* sp.

DATA

Date	May, 1993	Aquatic Plants	*Glossostigma elatinoides*
Aquarium	W22 x D22 x H22 (in)		*Cryptocoryne lucens*
Lighting	Halogen Lamp 150W x 1 unit, turned on for 12 hours		*Fontinalis antipyretica*
Filter	External Filter, Bio Rio		*Isoetes japonica*
Substrate	Oisosuna (Sea gravel), Power Sand, Bacter 100		*Riccia fluitans*
CO_2	Pollen Glass Beetle 40, 3 bubbles per second via CO_2 Beetle Counter		*Lagenandra thwaitesii*
			Vallisneria neotropicalis
Additives	Brighty K; Green Brighty STEP 3; Green Gain	Animals	*Sawbwa resplendens*
Water Change	1/3 once a week		*Taeniacara candidi*
Water Quality	Temperature 77°F; pH 6.8; TH 20mg/l		*Caridina japonica*
			Otocinclus **sp.**

DATA

Date	July, 1993
Aquarium	W24 x D12 x H14 (in)
Lighting	20W x 4 units, turned on for 11 hours
Filter	External Filter, Bio Rio
Substrate	Oisosuna (Sea gravel), Power Sand, Bacter 100
CO₂	Pollen Glass, 2 bubbles per second via CO₂ Bubble Counter
Additives	Brighty K; Green Brighty STEP 2
Water Change	1/3 once a week
Water Quality	Temperature 79°F; pH 6.8; TH 20mg/l
Aquatic Plants	*Riccia fluitans*
	Eleocharis acicularis
Animals	*Inpaichthys kerri*
	Caridina japonica
	Otocinclus sp.

DATA

Date	╱ September, 1993
Aquarium	╱ W24 x D12 x H14 (in)
Lighting	╱ 20W x 4 units, turned on for 9 hours
Filter	╱ External Filter, Bio Rio
Substrate	╱ Oisosuna (Sea gravel), Power Sand, Bacter 100
CO₂	╱ Pollen Glass, 2 bubbles per second via CO₂ Bubble Counter
Additives	╱ Brighty K; Green Brighty STEP 2
Water Change	╱ 1/3-1/2 once a week
Water Quality	╱ Temperature 79°F; pH 6.9; TH 50mg/l
Aquatic Plants	╱ *Marsilea crenata*
	Riccia fluitans
	Echinodorus tenellus
	Eleocharis acicularis
	Cyperus helferi
Animals	╱ *Tanichthys albonubes*
	Caridina japonica
	Otocinclus sp.

DATA

Date	╱ January 1992
Aquarium	╱ W24 x D12 x H14 (in)
Lighting	╱ 20W x 4 units, turned on for 12 hours
Filter	╱ External Filter, Bio Rio
Substrate	╱ Oisosuna (Sea gravel), Power Sand, Bacter 100
CO₂	╱ Pollen Glass, 2 bubbles per second via CO₂ Bubble Counter
Additives	╱ Brighty K; Green Brighty STEP 2
Water Change	╱ 1/3 once every 5 days
Water Quality	╱ Temperature 79°F; pH 6.9; TH 20mg/l
Aquatic Plants	╱ *Glossostigma elatinoides*
	Anubias barteri var. *nana*
	Riccia fluitans
	Eleocharis acicularis
	Sagittaria subulata
Animals	╱ *Pterophyllum scalare*
	Caridina japonica
	Otocinclus sp.

DATA

Date	╱September 1993
Aquarium	╱W24 x D12 x H14 (in)
Lighting	╱20W x 4 units, turned on for 12 hours
Filter	╱External Filter, Bio Rio, Bamboo Charcoal
Substrate	╱Oisosuna (Sea gravel), Power Sand
CO₂	╱Pollen Glass, 2 bubbles per second via CO₂ Bubble Counter
Additives	╱Brighty K; Green Brighty STEP 2; Green Gain; Green Bacter
Water Change	╱1/2 once a week
Water Quality	╱Temperature 77°F; pH 7.0; TH 50mg/l
Aquatic Plants	╱Glossostigma elatinoides

Glossostigma elatinoides
Hemianthus micranthemoides
Lagarosiphon madagascariensis
Rotala wallichii
Didiplis diandra
Micranthemum unbrosum
Rotala macrandra
Dorimalia cordata
Myriophyllum matogrossense
Myriophyllum hippuroides
Nesaea sp.
Eusteralis stellata
Eusteralis verticillata
Ludwigia ovaris
Amania gracilis
Bacopa caroliniana
Alternanthera reineckii

Animals ╱*Priapella intermedia*
Inpaichthys kerri
Caridina japonica
Otocinclus sp.

DATA

Date	╱ October 1993	Aquatic Plants ╱	*Cryptocoryne parva*
Aquarium	╱ W24 x D12 x H14 (in)		*Cryptocoryne cordata*
Lighting	╱ 20W x 4 units, turned on for 10 hours		*Cryptocoryne affinis*
Filter	╱ External Filter, Bio Rio, Bamboo Charcoal		*Cryptocoryne lucens*
Substrate	╱ Oisosuna (Sea gravel), Power Sand, Bacter 100,		*Cryptocoryne blassii*
	Clear Super, Iron Bottom		*Fontinalis antipyretica*
CO_2	╱ Pollen Glass, 2 bubbles per second via CO_2	Animals	╱ *Trigonostigma heteromorpha*
	Bubble Counter		*Caridina japonica*
Additives	╱ Brighty K; Green Brighty STEP 1; Green Gain		*Otocinclus sp.*
Water Change	╱ 1/2 once a week		
Water Quality	╱ Temperature 77°F; pH 6.8; TH 20mg/l		

The Essence of Nature Aquarium

What is the essence of a beautiful landscape? The compositional beauty produced by flora and other things may be a part of it, but isn't it ultimately a perfectly functioning ecosystem? It is, in fact, a balance. The world of aquarium is no exception. Therefore, I place the utmost importance on creating a balance in Nature Aquarium. The works of Nature Aquarium have not changed fundamentally over the years. I believe that they were highly refined from the start. There have not been any very large changes in the layouts since the question of "what type of environment would I prefer if I were a fish" was always at the base when the layouts were created. This is similar to the fact that nature retains the same appearance, or the fact that the core of an artist never changes whether the artist is a painter, a sculptor, or a calligrapher.

ADA holds the International Aquatic Plant Layout Contest every year. Every entry is the result of hard work, but there are some that appear overly technical. They might have employed too many techniques because they were created for the sake of the contest. However, I personally do not like a layout that does not look like a comfortable place for fish. I have been producing Nature Aquarium layouts for a long time. Some people criticize that I have run out of ideas and images or that all of my works have the same old pattern. I respond to such remarks by telling them, "Are you kidding? There is no such thing as the same old pattern in nature." Many a layout can be created by varying the design of the appearance, but if it departs from its essence, doing so is like overlooking the forest for the trees. I hope to keep on creating layouts that seem to truly recreate nature, and hopefully in a much larger aquarium that I have never experienced before in my life.

DATA

Date	September 1993
Aquarium	W71 x D63 x H35 (in)
Lighting	40W x 15 units, turned on for 12 hours
Filter	External Filter, Bio Rio, Bamboo Charcoal
Substrate	Oisosuna (Sea gravel), Power Sand, Bacter 100, Clear Super, Iron Bottom
CO₂	Pollen Glass Beetle 50 x 4 units, 5 bubbles per second via CO₂ Beetle Counter x 4 units
Additives	Brighty K; Green Brighty STEP 3; Green Gain
Water Change	1/2 once every three weeks
Water Quality	Temperature 79°F; pH 7.0; TH 20mg/l
Aquatic Plants	*Glossostigma elatinoides*
	Cyperus helferi
	Microsorum pteropus
	Echinodorus uruguaiensis
	Echinodorus horemanii
	Echinodorus rubin
	Najas sp.
	Riccia fluitans
	Eleocharis acicularis
	Isoetes japonica
	Cryptocoryne balansae
	Potamogeton oxyphyllus
Animals	*Pterophyllum scalare* var.
	Hemigrammopetersius caudalis
	Hemigrammus bleheri
	Caridina japonica
	Otocinclus sp.

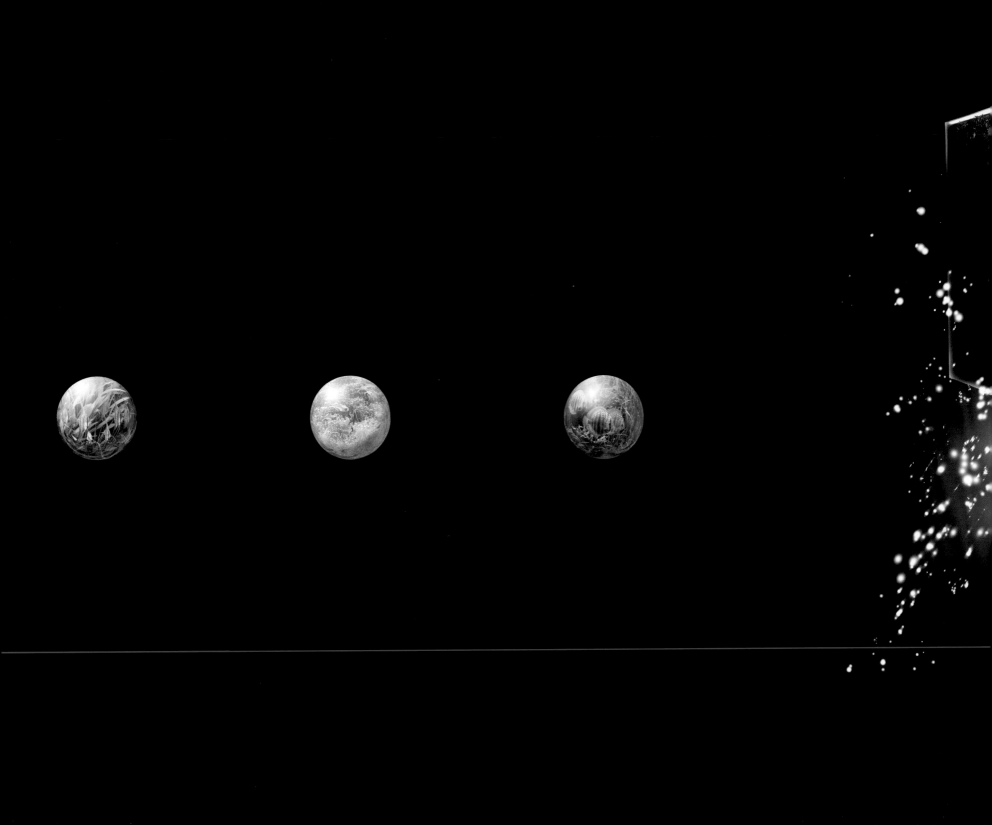

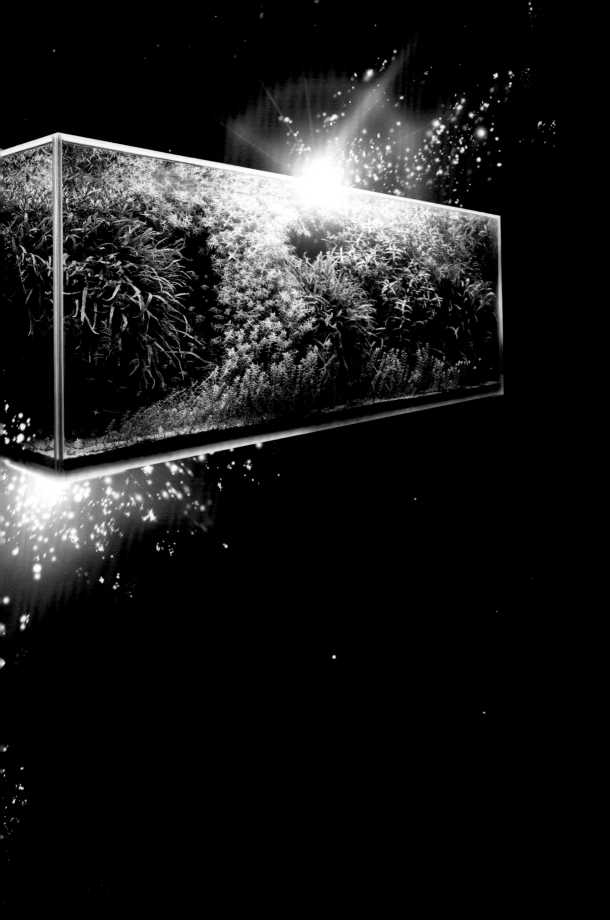

TAKASHI AMANO
NATURE AQUARIUM
COMPLETE WORKS

1994-1996

DATA
Date /April, 1994
Aquarium /W24 x D12 x H14 (in)
Lighting /NA Lamp 20W x 4 units, turned on for 10 hours
Filter /External Filter, Bio Rio, Bamboo Charcoal,
Palm Net
Substrate /Oisosuna (Sea gravel), Power Sand S,
Bacter 100, Growth Plate
CO₂ /Pollen Glass, 3 bubbles per second via CO₂
Bubble Counter
Aeration /14 hours after the light is turned off using
Lily Pipe P-2
Additives /Brighty K; Green Brighty STEP 2; Green Gain
Water Change /1/3 twice a week
Water Quality /Temperature 77°F; pH 6.8; TH 50mg/l
Aquatic Plants /Glossostigma elatinoides
Riccia fluitans
Eusteralis stellata
Animals /Pseudomugil furcatus
Caridina japonica
Otocinclus sp.

DATA
Date /May, 1994
Aquarium /W24 x D12 x H14 (in)
Lighting /NA Lamp 20W x 4 units, turned on for 10 hours
Filter /External Filter, Bio Rio, Bamboo Charcoal
Substrate /Oisosuna (Sea gravel), Power Sand S,
Bacter 100, Clear Super, Glowth Plate
CO₂ /Pollen Glass, 3 bubbles per second via CO₂
Bubble Counter
Aeration /14 hours after the light is turned off using
Lily Pipe P-2
Additives /Brighty K; Green Brighty STEP 2; Green Gain
Water Change /1/3 twice a week
Water Quality /Temperature 77°F; pH 6.8; TH 50mg/l
Aquatic Plants /Riccia fluitans
Echinodorus tenellus
Micranthemum unbrosum
Cyperus helferi
Fontinalis antipyretica
Crinum calamistratum
Hemianthus micranthemoides var.
Hydrocotyle maritima
Rotala wallichii
Rotala macrandra sp.
Limnophila aquatica
Amania gracilis
Myriophyllum propinquum
Echinodorus amazonicus
Echinodorus osiris
Echinodorus rubin
Animals /Poecilia reticulata var.
Caridina japonica
Otocinclus sp.

DATA

Date	/May 1995
Aquarium	/W24 x D12 x H14 (cm)
Lighting	/NA Lamp 20W x 4 units, turned on for 10 hours
Filter	/External Filter, Bio Rio, Bamboo Charcoal, Palm Net
Substrate	/Oisosuna (Sea gravel), Power Sand S, Bacter 100, Clear Super
CO₂	/Pollen Glass, 2 bubbles per second via CO₂ Bubble Counter
Aeration	/14 hours after the light is turned off using Lily Pipe P-2
Additives	/Brighty K; Green Brighty STEP 2; Green Gain

Water Change／1/3 twice a week
Water Quality／Temperature 77°F pH 6.8, TH 50mg/l
Aquatic Plants／*Riccia fluitans*
Echinodorus tenellus
Hydrocotyle maritima
Hydrocotyle verticillata
Cryptocoryne wendtii (green)
Cryptocoryne wendtii (brown)
Cryptocoryne bullosa
Dorimalia cordata var.

Cyperus helferi
Echinodorus rubin
Lagarosiphon madagascariensis
Hygrophila polysperma
Rotala macrandra sp.
Ludwigia arcuata
Animals／*Thoracocharax stellatus*
Hemigrammus armstrongi
Caridina japonica
Otocinclus sp.

DATA

Date   ／August 1994
Aquarium／W47 x D18 x H18 (in)
Lighting ／NA Lamp 20W x 10 units, turned on for 10 hours
Filter   ／External Filter, Bio Rio, Bamboo Charcoal, Palm Net
Substrate／Oisosuna (Sea gravel), Power Sand Special M,
             Bacter 100, Clear Super
CO₂   ／Pollen Glass Beetle 40 x 2 units, 2 bubbles per second
             via CO₂ Beetle Counter x 2 units
Aeration ／14 hours after the light is turned off using Lily Pipe P-4
Additives／Brighty K; Green Brighty STEP 2

Water Change／1/3 twice a week
Water Quality ／Temperature 77°F; pH 6.8; TH 50mg/l
Aquatic Plants／*Glossostigma elatinoides*
                  Riccia fluitans
                  Eleocharis acicularis
                  Hemianthus micranthemoides
                  Fontinalis antipyretica
                  Bolbitis heudelotii
                  Aponogeton rigidifolius

Animals／*Hemigrammus erythrozonus*
          Caridina japonica
          Otocinclus sp.

DATA

Date	November 1994	CO₂	Pollen Glass Beetle 30 × 2 units, 2 bubbles per	Aquatic Plants	*Limnophila aquatica*	Animals	*Hemigrammus hyanuary*
Aquarium	W35 × D18 × H18 (in)		second via CO₂ Beetle Counter × 2 units		*Lagarosiphon madagascariensis*		*Hyphessobrycon erythrostigma*
Lighting	NA Lamp 20W × 8 units, turned on for 10 hours	Aeration	14 hours after the light is turned off using Lily Pipe P-4		*Eusteralis stellata*		*Hemigrammus erythrozonus*
Filter	External Filter, Bio Rio, Bamboo Charcoal, Palm Net	Additives	Brighty K; Green Brighty Special LIGHTS		*Bacopa caroliniana*		*Thoracocharax stellatus*
Substrate	Oisosuna (Sea gravel), Power Sand Special M,	Water Change	1/3 twice a week		*Riccia fluitans*		*Colisa lalia* var.
	Bacter 100, Growth Plate	Water Quality	Temperature 77°F; pH 6.8; TH 50mg/l		*Eleocharis acicularis*		*Caridina japonica*
							Otocinclus sp.

The Real Pleasure of Keeping Discus in a Large Aquarium

Although the vividly colored hybrid discus is attractive, the wild original species also has a big appeal. Generally speaking, the wild strain is more timid than its artificially bred hybrid counterpart. It tends to calm down better if an aquarium offers driftwood and aquatic plants where it can seek refuge. It becomes accustomed to a new environment and settles down more quickly if its environmental condition is kept as similar to the natural habitat as possible. For this reason, Nature Aquarium created in a large aquarium is more suitable for wild discus. However, keeping discus in a layout has its own difficulties.

When a discus is introduced in an aquarium at first, it hides behind driftwood and does not come out to swim gracefully in an aquarium. Under such conditions, its body color darkens to blend into the shade. Although feeding can sometimes be effective for getting it acclimated to the aquarium environment as quickly as possible, it does not take well to artificially prepared food initially. It may be necessary to devise some special measures to entice them, such as giving some bloodworms along with prepared food at the risk of fouling water, or putting other fish in the aquarium in the hope that discus will follow them to come out of hiding. After overcoming many difficulties and becoming accustomed to the aquarium environment, a discus not only graces the aquarium by regaining its beautiful colors, but it also starts to show its natural behaviors, such as spawning on driftwood. That will greatly add to the joy of keeping this fish. The real pleasure of keeping wild discus in Nature Aquarium is to bring out their natural beauty and behaviors by perfecting the habitat environment in an aquarium.

DATA

Date	November 1994
Aquarium	W71 x D39 x H31.5 (in)
Lighting	NA Lamp 40W x 4 units, NA Lamp 20W x 14 units, turned on for 10 hours
Filter	External Filter, Bio Rio, Bamboo Charcoal, Palm Net
Substrate	Oisosuna (Sea gravel), Power Sand L, Bacter 100, Clear Super
CO$_2$	Pollen Glass Beetle 50 x 2 units, 5 bubbles per second via CO$_2$ Beetle Counter x 2 units
Aeration	14 hours after the light is turned off with NA Control Timer
Additives	Brighty K; Green Gain
Water Change	1/3 twice a week
Water Quality	Temperature 77°F; pH 7.3; TH 50mg/l
Aquatic Plants	*Bolbitis heudelotii*
	Fontinalis antipyretica
	Echinodorus tenellus
	Echinodorus uruguaiensis
	Cryptocoryne wendtii (green)
	Cryptocoryne wendtii (brown)
	Cryptocoryne wendtii (Mi Oya)
	Cryptocoryne lucens
	Cryptocoryne balansae
	Sagittaria subulata
	Vallisneria neotropicalis
	Cyperus helferi
	Aponogeton ulvaceus
	Nymphaea lotus rubra
Animals	*Thoracocharax stellatus*
	Hemigrammus bleheri
	Tetragonopterus argenteus
	Symphysodon aequifasciata var.
	Caridina japonica
	Otocinclus sp.

DATA

		Aquatic Plants	/ *Echinodorus tenellus*	*Hygrophila polysperma*

Date ╱ January, 1995

Aquarium ╱ W47 x D18 x H18 (in)

Lighting ╱ NA Lamp 20W x 12 units, turned on for 10 hours

Filter ╱ External Filter, Bio Rio, Bamboo Charcoal, Palm Net

Substrate ╱ Oisosuna (Sea gravel), Power Sand Special M,
Bacter 100, Clear Super

CO₂ ╱ Pollen Glass Beetle 50, 5 bubbles per second via CO₂
Beetle Counter

Aeration ╱ 14 hours after the light is turned off using Lily Pipe P-4

Additives ╱ Brighty K; Green Brighty Special SHADE

Water Change ╱ 1/4 once a week

Water Quality ╱ Temperature 77ºF; pH 6.8; TH 50mg/l

Aquatic Plants ╱ *Echinodorus tenellus*
Sagittaria subulata var. *pusilla*
Riccia fluitans
Isoetes japonica
Microsorum pteropus
Cryptocoryne wendtii (brown)
Cryptocoryne walkeri var. *lutea*
Cryptocoryne undulata (BL)
Cryptocoryne petchii
Cryptocoryne lucens
Cryptocoryne undulata
Cryptocoryne retrospiralis

Hygrophila polysperma
Sagittaria subulata
Vallisneria neotropicalis
Lysimachia nummularia var. *aurea*
Hygrophila lacustrus
Ludwigia arcuata
Aponogeton ulvaceus
Nymphaea lotus rubra
Hygrophila stricta

Animals ╱ *Trigonostigma heteromorpha*
Caridina japonica
Otocinclus sp.

Combining Aquatic Plants and Fish That Come From the Same Area

People occasionally ask me for criteria for selecting types of fish that go well with an aquascape. I often answer by saying "gorillas don't live in a wide open savanna and zebras are not found in a dense jungle." Those asking usually look puzzled at this response, but my idea is this: the shape and behavior of an animal are often the results of the unique development that enabled it to adapt to the environmental conditions of its habitat. Therefore, I find it strange to ignore the natural order between an animal and its habitat. In other words, fish in the family of Betta prefer to live in a small pool of water or an area with a slow water flow, and the

Black Phantom Tetra that swims with fluttering movement goes together well with stem plant bushes, and fast swimming fish with a slender body shapes match an Iwagumi layout that resembles a vast grassland, where water current circulates well.

The compatibility of an aquascape and fish sets a basic guideline for combining aquatic plants and selecting fish for a layout. A pairing of *Cryptocoryne* and *Rasbora* from the same area is a good example of a well-matched combination of aquatic plants and fish. *Cryptocoryne* and *Rasbora*, both of which are representative of Southeast Asia, come in many varieties and are distributed over a large area. Therefore, they may not necessarily live in the same river or area naturally, but they go together inexplicably well, possi-

bly because of the similar climate of their habitats. Although the colors of the leaves of plants in the *Cryptocoryne* family vary from green to brown, depending on the types and the growing environment, their tones are quite similar. This works well with the colors of rasboras. Similarly, Southeast Asian stem plants in the *Hygrophila* family also go together well with rasboras. These aquatic plants, when used primarily, create an aquascape with a strong Southeast Asian feature that goes together well with fishes in the rasbora family, even if some aquatic plants from different areas are added to the mix.

DATA

Date	March, 1995	Aquatic Plants	*Glossostigma elatinoides*
Aquarium	W24 x D12 x H14 (in)		*Anubias barteri* **var.** *nana* **"narrow"**
Lighting	NA Lamp 20W x 4 units, turned on for 10 hours	Animals	*Melanotaenia praecox*
Filter	External Filter, Bio Rio, Bamboo Charcoal, Palm Net		*Caridina japonica*
Substrate	Oisosuna (Sea gravel), Power Sand S, Bacter 100, Clear Super		*Otocinclus* **sp.**
CO₂	Pollen Glass, 2 bubbles per second via CO₂ Bubble Counter		
Aeration	14 hours after the light is turned off using Pollen Glass for AIR with NA Control Timer		
Additives	Brighty K; Green Brighty STEP 1; ECA		
Water Change	1/3 once a week		
Water Quality	Temperature 77°F; pH 7.0; TH 50mg/l		

DATA
Date / April, 1995
Aquarium / W22 x D22 x H22 (cm)
Lighting / Halogen Lamp 150W x 1 unit, turned on for 12 hours
Filter / External Filter, Bio Rio, Bamboo Charcoal, Palm Net
Substrate / Oisosuna (Sea gravel), Power Sand M, Bacter 100, Clear Super
CO₂ / Pollen Glass Beetle 40, 4 bubbles per second via CO₂ Beetle Counter
Aeration / 12 hours after the light is turned off using Lily Pipe P-4
Additives / Brighty K; Green Brighty STEP 2; Green Bacter
Water Change / 1/3 once a week
Water Quality / Temperature 75°F; pH 6.9; TH 50mg/l
Aquatic Plants / *Fontinalis antipyretica*
Riccia fluitans
Hemianthus micranthemoides
Hemianthus micranthemoides var.
Cryptocoryne wendtii (green)
Cryptocoryne wendtii (brown)
Cryptocoryne beckettii
Cryptocoryne retrospiralis
Cryptocoryne costata
Cryptocoryne pontederifolia
Animals / *Trigonostigma heteromorpha*
Puntius gerius
Caridina japonica
Otocinclus sp.

DATA
Date / April, 1995
Aquarium / W16 x D16 x H16 (in)
Lighting / 27W(Twin) x 4 units, turned on for 8 hours
Filter / External Filter, Bio Rio, Bamboo Charcoal, Palm Net
Substrate / Oisosuna (Sea gravel), Power Sand M,
Bacter 100, Clear Super
CO₂ / Pollen Glass, 2 bubbles per second via CO₂
Bubble Counter
Aeration / 16 hours after the light is turned off using Pollen
Glass for AIR with NA Control Timer
Additives / Brighty K; Green Brighty Special SHADE; Phyton Git
Water Change / 1/3 once a week
Water Quality / Temperature 75°F; pH 6.9; TH 50mg/l
Aquatic Plants / *Marsilea crenata*
Anubias barteri var. *nana* "narrow"
Anubias barteri var. *nana* "wrinkle"
Cryptocoryne retrospiralis
Cryptocoryne costata
Cryptocoryne sp.
Bolbitis heudelotii
Fontinalis antipyretica
Animals / *Aplocheilichthys narmani*
Caridina japonica
Otocinclus sp.

DATA

Date	／August, 1995
Aquarium	／W71 x D39 x H31.5 (in)
Lighting	／NA Lamp 40W x 4 units, NA Lamp 20W x 14 units, turned on for 10 hours
Filter	／External Filter, Bio Cube 20, NA Carbon
Substrate	／Oisosuna (Sea gravel), Power Sand L, Bacter 100, Clear Super
CO_2	／Pollen Glass Beetle 50 x 2 units, 3 bubbles per second via CO_2 Beetle Counter x 2 units
Aeration	／14 hours after the light is turned off with NA Control Timer
Additives	／Brighty K; Green Brighty Special SHADE; Green Gain
Water Change	／1/3 once a week
Water Quality	／Temperature 77°F; pH 6.5; TH 50mg/l

Aquatic Plants ／*Echinodorus tenellus*
Sagittaria subulata var. *pusilla*
Anubias barteri var. *nana*
Sagittaria subulata
Echinodorus osiris "rose"
Bolbitis heudelotii
Cryptocoryne balansae
Vallisneria neotropicalis
Hygrophila lacustrus

Animals ／*Paracheirodon axelrodi*
Caridina japonica
Otocinclus sp.

Composition and Shading of Nature

It is important to know the composition of nature in order to develop a three dimensional layout in Nature Aquarium. Whether it is a layout with driftwood in the image of a dense jungle or a simple Iwagumi layout, I learned the compositions of nature with my own eyes, standing in such a place in nature or by taking a photograph of it.

I judge the mastery levels of a layout, or a picture for that matter, by its framework. In the case of an animal in particular, it is important to have an accurate understanding of its bone structure. Even when the outline of a body is drawn well, its bone structure appears unnatural in some cases. Similarly, there is a framework in a layout. Whether the framework appears natural or not will determine the quality of a layout. In a layout with driftwood, driftwood serves as the framework of the layout and prevents aquatic plants from spreading too much, or it works as a guideline for trimming to maintain the composition, although the driftwood may not be very visible buried in aquatic plants.

When it comes to light, I use backlight on purpose to pronounce a shaded area in a photograph. In a landscape photograph, a spatial effect and depth can be expressed with light and dark contrast. The combination of light and shade is important when creating a layout as well. In particular, the use of shadows can make or break a layout. Old flower garden style layouts were generally made up solely with light areas. They were often featureless and compositionally uninteresting. Having shade is desirable from an ecological standpoint as well, since fish have no place to hide if there isn't any shade. In Nature Aquarium, shadows are added to a layout by creating shaded areas with composition materials, such as rocks and driftwood, and planting sciophytes, such as mosses and ferns. Such an idea does not seem to be prevalent in Europe. However, it is natural to have shadows in a three dimensional world.

DATA

Date	December, 1995
Aquarium	W71 x D24 x H24 (in)
Lighting	20W x 24 units, turned on for 10 hours
Filter	External Filter, Bio Rio, Bamboo Charcoal, Palm Net
Substrate	Oisosuna (Sea gravel), Power Sand L, Bacter 100, Clear Super
CO_2	Pollen Glass Beetle 50 x 2 units, 2 bubbles per second via
	CO_2 Beetle Counter x 2 units
Aeration	14 hours after the light is turned off via Lily Pipe P-6
Additives	Brighty K; Green Bacter
Water Change	1/3 twice a week
Water Quality	Temperature 79°F; pH 7.0; TH 50mg/l

Aquatic Plants	*Fontinalis antipyretica*
Animals	*Pterophyllum altum*
	Caridina japonica
	Otocinclus sp.

The Compatibility of Driftwood and Angelfish

I am occasionally asked if driftwood or rocks are necessary for an aquatic plant layout. I have to simply answer "it's up to your own imagination." I use composition materials, such as driftwood or rocks, 99% of the time in Nature Aquarium layouts that I create. Even if it is a type of composition in which the materials are hidden by aquatic plants, composition materials play an important role as the framework of a layout, and they also serve an important source of inspiration. For example, the drama of a living organism

that took place in order for it to reach its final form is hidden in a piece of driftwood. How you perceive and express it becomes an important point.

It was when I was taking photographs underwater in the Negro river in the Amazon that I saw something very memorable that revealed the relationship between driftwood and fish in nature. During the rainy season, a large number of fallen trees float down the river from upstream and eventually become shelters for various fishes. I saw a school of angelfish along the shore where the drift-

wood collected. The water of the Negro river is a clear, brownish-red. To my surprise, the characteristic stripes of the angelfish blended in the silhouettes of driftwood perfectly, and the fish were totally obscured in the water. The compressed body shape and fins that can collapse to change their heights must have evolved from the necessity of passing through narrow spaces between pieces of driftwood. I have often thought that driftwood and angel-fish go together well. This incident convinced me that it was based on natural ecology after all.

I have visited various waters of the Amazon, Southeast Asia, and West Africa in the past and have seen driftwood that had become a hiding place for fish and a place for mosses and ferns to grow on. I often use driftwood in the middle ground of an aquatic plant layout as a place for fish to seek refuge in and the locations to which I attach mosses and ferns. Such an expression renders a natural feel which actually matches the way driftwood exists in nature.

DATA

Date	/January, 1995	
Aquarium	/W47 x D18 x H18 (in)	
Lighting	/NA Lamp 20W x 8 units, 40W x 1 unit, turned on for 10 hours	
Filter	/External Filter, Bio Rio, Bamboo Charcoal, Palm Net	
Substrate	/Oisosuna (Sea gravel), Power Sand Special M, Bacter 100, Clear Super	
CO_2	/Pollen Glass Beetle 50, 5 bubbles per second via CO_2 Beetle Counter	
Aeration	/14 hours after the light is turned off via Lily Pipe P-4	
Additives	/Brighty K; Green Brighty Special SHADE	
Water Change	/1/4 once a week	
Water Quality	/Temperature 76°F; pH 7.0; TH 50mg/l	

Aquatic Plants / *Cryptocoryne pontederifolia*
Cryptocoryne undulata
Cryptocoryne balansae
Cryptocoryne undulata "BL"
Cryptocoryne petchii
Cryptocoryne blassii
Cryptocoryne wendtii (green)
Echinodorus tenellus
Eleocharis acicularis
Fontinalis antipyretica

Animals / *Puntius gerius*
Trigonostigma espei
Rasbora pauciperforata
Rasbora dorsiocellata macrophthalma
Rasbora borapetensis
Rasbora sp.
Caridina japonica
Otocinclus sp.

DATA

Date	╱December, 1996
Aquarium	╱W35 x D18 x H18 (in)
Lighting	╱NA Lamp 32W x 6 units, turned on for 10 hours
Filter	╱External Filter, Bio Rio, Bamboo Charcoal, Palm Net
Substrate	╱Aqua Soil Amazonia, Power Sand M, Bacter 100, Clear Super
CO$_2$	╱Pollen Glass Beetle 40, 3 bubbles per second via CO$_2$ Beetle Counter
Aeration	╱14 hours after the light is turned off using Pollen Glass Beetle 40 for AIR with NA Control Timer
Additives	╱Brighty K; Green Brighty STEP 2
Water Change	╱1/2 twice a week
Water Quality	╱Temperature 77°F; pH 6.8; TH 20mg/l
Aquatic Plants	╱*Echinodorus tenellus*
	Echinodorus sp.
	Echinodorus uruguaiensis
Animals	╱*Iguanodectes spilurus*
	Caridina japonica
	Otocinclus sp.

DATA

Date	April, 1996	Aquatic Plants	*Glossostigma elatinoides*	Animals	*Ladigesia roloffi*

Date   April, 1996

Aquarium   W47 x D18 x H18 (in)

Lighting   NA Lamp 20W x 12 units, turned on for 10 hours

Filter   External Filter, Bio Cube 20, NA Carbon

Substrate   Aqua Soil Africana, Power Sand M, Bacter 100, Clear Super

CO₂   Pollen Glass Beetle 50, 3 bubbles per second via CO₂ Beetle Counter

Aeration   14 hours after the light is turned off via Lily Pipe P-6

Additives   Brighty K; ECA

Water Change   1/3 twice a week

Water Quality   Temperature 77°F; pH 6.8; TH 10mg/l

Aquatic Plants

Glossostigma elatinoides
Lilaeopsis novae-zelandiae
Anubias barteri var. *nana*
Anubias barteri var. *nana* (narrow)
Sagittaria subulata var. *pusilla*
Hydrocotyle maritima

Animals

Ladigesia roloffi
Pelvicachromis taeniatus "Dehane"
Pelvicachromis taeniatus "Kienke"
Pelvicachromis taeniatus "Nigeria red"
Anomalochromis thomasi
Caridina japonica
Otocinclus sp.

Anubias That I Found in West Africa

There are groups of aquatic plants that represent certain regions, such as *Echinodorus* of the Amazon and *Cryptocoryne* of Southeast Asia. The family of *Anubias* is a group of aquatic plants that represents West Africa. These plants, such as *Anubias nana*, are frequently used in Nature Aquarium. The plants in the Anubias family were something that I never tried until about fifteen years ago because of a silly prejudice. However, I happened to notice that *Anubias* plants could attach and grow well on driftwood and rocks, although they did not do well when

planted in the substrate. This got me interested in finding what kind of environment *Anubias* grows in naturally. Although *Anubias* were generally known to grow naturally in West Africa, how they grew and in what kind of places was a mystery. Suddenly a piece of information came that a German ichthyologist knew a place where *Anubias* grew naturally. I decided to go to Gabonese Republic in West Africa based on the information.

The tropical rainforest of West Africa has an extremely hot and humid climate. The maximum temperature rises above 104ºF daily and its humidity is always 100%. Dangerous wild animals

roam the jungle where aquatic plants grow. It is also known as a dangerous area plagued by contagious diseases, such as malaria, yellow fever, and Ebola hemorrhagic fever. Overcome by the desire to look at their natural habitat, I went down the trails of the jungle with a local Pygmy as a guide. Food was in short supply, and the temperature difference of night and day was great in the jungle. This temperature difference was tough on my weakened body. I was told beforehand that one can get ill simply by getting into the water in some areas, but I could not help but drink the water from the stream at my feet out of severe

thirst. The water tasted better than any famous spring water that I could buy in convenience stores in Japan.

By the time we reached the river where *Anubias* grew, I was at the limit of my physical strength. But as soon as I stood at the river bank, I felt liberated from my fatigue and was filled with a great joy and excitement. *Anubias* plants were growing densely, clinging tightly to rocks and driftwood on the bank, just like they were in my aquarium. Going into the field is fun because of such a discovery.

DATA

Date	/February, 1996
Aquarium	/W35 x D18 x H18 (in)
Lighting	/NA Lamp 30W x 5 units, turned on for 10 hours
Filter	/External Filter, Bio Rio, Bamboo Charcoal, Palm Net
Substrate	/Oisosuna (Sea gravel), Power Sand M, Bacter 100, Clear Super
CO_2	/Pollen Glass Beetle 40, 3 bubbles per second using CO_2 Beetle Counter
Aeration	/14 hours after the light is turned off via Pollen Glass Beetle 40 for AIR with NA Control Timer
Additives	/Brighty K; Green Brighty STEP 2; Phyton Git; ECA

Water Change	/1/2 twice a week
Water Quality	/Temperature 77°F; pH 6.8; TH 20mg/l
Aquatic Plants	/*Glossostigma elatinoides*
	Riccia fluitans
	Fontinalis antipyretica
	Microsorum pteropus
	Hygrophila stricta
Animals	/*Nematobrycon palmeri*
	Caridina japonica
	Otocinclus sp.

DATA

Date	/October, 1996	Aquatic Plants	/*Marsilea crenata*
Aquarium	/W35 x D18 x H18 (in)		*Riccia fluitans*
Lighting	/NA Lamp 30W x 5 units, turned on for 10 hours		*Fontinalis antipyretica*
Filter	/External Filter, Bio Rio, Bamboo Charcoal, Palm Net		*Eleocharis acicularis*
Substrate	/Oisosuna (Sea gravel), Power Sand M, Bacter 100,		*Anubias barteri* var. *nana* (narrow)
	Clear Super		*Cryptocoryne parva*
CO_2	/Pollen Glass Beetle 40, 2 bubbles per second via CO_2		*Cryptocoryne undulata*
	Beetle Counter		*Cryptocoryne balansae*
Aeration	/14 hours after the light is turned off using Pollen Glass	Animals	/*Rasbora dorsiocellata macrophthalma*
	Beetle 40 for AIR with NA Control Timer		*Sphaerichthys osphromenoides*
Additives	/Brighty K; Green Brighty STEP 2; Green Gain; ECA		*Caridina japonica*
Water Change	/1/3 once every two weeks		*Otocinclus* sp.
Water Quality	/Temperature 75°F; pH 7.0; TH 20mg/l		

DATA

Date	April, 1995
Aquarium	W24 x D12 x H14 (in)
Lighting	NA Lamp 20W x 4 units, turned on for 10 hours
Filter	External Filter, Bio Rio, Bamboo Charcoal, Palm Net
Substrate	Aqua Soil Amazonia, Power Sand Special S, Bacter 100, Clear Super, Iron Bottom
CO₂	Pollen Glass, 2 bubbles per second via CO₂ Bubble Counter
Aeration	14 hours after the light is turned off using Pollen Glass for AIR with NA Control Timer
Additives	Brighty K; Green Gain; ECA
Water Change	1/3 twice a week
Water Quality	Temperature 77°F; pH 6.6; TH 10mg/l or less
Aquatic Plants	*Marsilea crenata*
	Cryptocoryne wendtii (Green)
	Cryptocoryne wendtii (Brown)
	Cryptocoryne wendtii (MiOya)
	Cryptocoryne wendtii var. *nevillii*
	Anubias barteri var. *nana (Narrow)*
	Cryptocoryne balansae
Animals	*Puntius oligolepis*
	Rasbora borapetensis
	Caridina japonica
	Otocinclus sp.

DATA

Date	April, 1995
Aquarium	W24 x D12 x H14 (in)
Lighting	NA Lamp 20W x 4 units, turned on for 10 hours
Filter	External Filter, Bio Rio, Bamboo Charcoal, Palm Net
Substrate	Aqua Soil Amazonia, Power Sand Special S, Bacter 100, Clear Super, Iron Bottom
CO₂	Pollen Glass, 2 bubbles per second via CO₂ Bubble Counter
Aeration	14 hours after the light is turned off using Pollen Glass for AIR with NA Control Timer
Additives	Brighty K; Green Brighty STEP 3; Phyton Git
Water Change	1/3 once a week
Water Quality	Temperature 79°F; pH 6.9; TH 50mg/l
Aquatic Plants	*Marsilea crenata*
	Cryptocoryne nevillii
	Cryptocoryne willisii
	Cryptocoryne petchii
	Cryptocoryne costata
	Cryptocoryne balansae
	Cryptocoryne wendtii var.
	Anubias barteri var. *nana*
	Anubias barteri var. *nana*
	Hemianthus micranthemoides var.
	Sagittaria subulata var. *pusilla*
	Lagarosiphon madagascariensis
Animals	*Aplocheilichthys narmani*
	Rasbora bankanensis
	Otocinclus sp.
	Caridina japonica

DATA

		Aquatic Plants	/Marsilea crenata
Date	/April, 1995		*Fontinalis antipyretica*
Aquarium	/W24 x D12 x H14 (in)		*Cryptocoryne wendtii* (brown)
Lighting	/NA Lamp 20W x 4 units, turned on for 10 hours		*Cryptocoryne wendtii* (Mi Oya)
Filter	/External Filter, Bio Rio, Bamboo Charcoal, Palm Net		*Cryptocoryne costata*
Substrate	/Oisosuna (Sea gravel), Power Sand Special S, Bacter 100, Clear Super		*Cryptocoryne walkeri* var. *legroi*
CO₂	/Pollen Glass, 2 bubbles per second via CO₂ Bubble Counter		*Cryptocoryne balansae*
Aeration	/14 hours after the light is turned off using Pollen Glass for AIR with NA Control Timer		*Cryptocoryne retrospiralis*
Additives	/Brighty K; Green Brighty Special SHADE; ECA	Animals	/*Rasboroides vaterifloris*
Water Change	/1/3 twice a week		*Caridina japonica*
Water Quality	/Temperature 77°F; pH 6.8; TH 50mg/l or less		*Otocinclus* sp.

DATA

		Aquatic Plants	/ Eusteralis stellata		Anubias barteri var. barteri

Date   / December, 1996

Aquarium   / W71 x D24 x H24 (in)

Lighting   / NA Lamp 20W x 24 units, turned on for 10 hours

Filter   / External Filter, Bio Rio, Bamboo Charcoal, Palm Net

Substrate   / Aqua Soil Amazonia, Power Sand L, Bacter 100,
              Clear Super

CO₂   / Pollen Glass Beetle 50, 5 bubbles per second via CO₂
              Beetle Counter

Aeration   / 14 hours after the light is turned off using Pollen
              Glass Beetle 50 for AIR with NA Control Timer

Additives   / Brighty K; ECA

Water Change / 1/4-1/3 once a week

Water Quality / Temperature 77°F; pH 7.0; TH 20mg/l

Aquatic Plants / *Eusteralis stellata*
Rotala macranda sp.
Rotala macranda
Rotala wallichii
Ludwigia peruensis
Rotala sp.
Eichhornia diversifolia
Micranthemum unbrosum
Eusteralis stellata
Micranthemum micranthemoides
Limnophila aquatica
Blyxa auberti
Marsilea crenata
Eleocharis acicularis
Anubias barteri var. *nana*

Anubias barteri var. *barteri*
Anubias congensis
Sagittaria subulata
Cryptocoryne wendtii (brown)
Cryptocoryne wendtii (Mi Oya)
Fontinalis antipyretica
Microsorum pteropus
Bolbitis heudelotii

Animals / *Pterophyllum altum*
Moenkhausia pittieri
Nematobrycon palmeri
Hemigrammus bleheri
Caridina japonica
Otocinclus sp.

To Promote Aquatic Plant Layouts

There are many things in the world that textbook theories cannot explain. Before Nature Aquarium was established, even one college professor flatly dismissed the concept of putting carbon dioxide into an aquarium instead of oxygen as a silly idea. By some quirk of fate when down and out, both financially and mentally, and ready to give up, I poured soda water into an aquarium out of idle curiosity. Declining aquatic plants started forming bubbles at once through photosynthesis. The delivery of carbon dioxide that no one believed in was brought to life by practice rather than by theory.

However, in order to popularize an aquatic plant layout, it was necessary to develop an easy-to-use, reliable lighting system and a substrate building method in addition to a CO_2 injection system. The product development thus started was very much like groping in the dark, and I had so many failures that I thought there was no one in the world who failed as much as I did. I suffered so many setbacks, but I had to put myself into a fish's position and develop the life support system for the fish, which used to live freely in a natural environment (including farmed fish), that I confined into a totally isolated environment. I thought that doing so was my responsibility and an ethical thing to do at the very least.

Today there are many systems that recreate an ecosystem, and the demand for aquariums as part of interior design is increasing. Some are placed in restaurants and hospital waiting rooms for their aesthetic values and therapeutic effects. In order to provide enjoyment to as many people as possible, special considerations must be given in order to meet the need of the viewers. For example, an aquarium placed in a hospital should not be too dark and depressing, and the composition must be adjusted by taking into considerations the movements of people around the aquarium and the location of doors in the area, instead of putting one's own preferences first. Such efforts will bring a refinement to a Nature Aquarium layout and widen its possibilities further.

DATA

		Aquatic Plants		Animals	
Date	December, 1996		*Eleocharis acicularis*		*Rasbora heteromorpha*
Aquarium	W94.5 x D24 x H24 (in)		*Cryptocoryne wendtii* **(green)**		*Caridina japonica*
Lighting	110W x 4 units, turned on for 10 hours		*Cryptocoryne wendtii* **(brown)**		*Otocinclus* **sp.**
Filter	Original External Filter, Bio Rio		*Cryptocoryne wendtii* **(tropica)**		
Substrate	Oisosuna (Sea gravel), Power Sand Special L,		*Cryptocoryne wendtii* **(Mi Oya)**		
	Bacter 100, Clear Super		*Cryptocoryne beckettii*		
CO₂	Pollen Glass Beetle 50 x 2 units, 4 bubbles per		*Cryptocoryne petchii*		
	second via CO₂ Beetle Counter x 2 units		*Cryptocoryne lucens*		
Aeration	14 hours after the light is turned off using Pollen		*Cryptocoryne costata*		
	Glass Beetle 50 for AIR with NA Control Timer		*Cryptocoryne wendtii* **var.**		
Additives	Brighty K; Green Brighty STEP 2		*Cryptocoryne wendtii* **var.**		
Water Change	1/2 once a week		*Cryptocoryne wendtii* **var.**		
Water Quality	Temperature 77°F; pH 6.8; TH 50mg/l		*Cryptocoryne wendtii* **var.**		

The Appearance of *Cryptocoryne* in Its Natural Habitat

Heading south by a car for a little over four hours from Phuket in Thailand, the scenery begins to take on a characteristically tropical air. It was about ten years ago that I visited the natural habitat of *Cryptocoryne* for the first time. I found plenty of ferns and mosses in the highlands of Borneo that I visited previously, but I saw practically no *Cryptocoryne* or stem plants (although I saw a lot of them in Sarawak.) I had high expectations this time since this was the area that Mr. Windelov of the plant farm, Tropica, in Denmark, had recommended as the best place for *Cryptocoryne* colonies. We finally came upon a spring-fed pond that looked like a blue, bottomless bog with nothing visible in the center. However, a giant, scaly shadow began to appear on the dark, eerie bottom of

the pond toward the downstream. It was a large colony of *Cryptocoryne* that I have been looking for. Overlapping like fish scales was *C. siamensis*. They were all healthy plants, with the back of their leaves glistening in reddish-purple color. I thoroughly enjoyed the wild beauty of the plants.

After finding out about their growing habits in their natural habitat, I began to think that there were a number of errors in the common growing practice of *Cryptocoryne* (especially the red broad leaf type.) The natural habitats of the plants in the *Cryptocoryne* family vary greatly. There are sciophytic types with round leaves that grow in a dark jungle where they barely receive any light, and there are heliophytic ones with narrow leaves that grow in a strong current where the sun shines on them all day long.

Although *Cryptocoryne* was generally considered as a type of plant that reacted sensitively to light intensity and did poorly in an aquarium, understanding the environment of its natural habitat makes it easier to grow this plant. *Cryptocoryne* tends to grow better in a mature substrate well-colonized by bacteria. The fact that it does not require frequent trimming like stem plants is appealing. It is a plant perfect for an aquascape that is to be maintained long term since it adapts well to an aquarium that has been kept for a long time and is easy to maintain. I recommend an aquascape made with *Cryptocoryne* if you find frequent trimming to be too much trouble, if you want to reduce the weekly water changes to once a month, or if your color preference changes from bright colors to subdued colors.

DATA

Date	/December, 1996
Aquarium	/W138 x D29.5 x H29.5 (in)
Lighting	/NA Lamp 40W x 9 units, NA Lamp 20W x 4 units, turned on for 10 hours
Filter	/External Filter, Bio Rio
Substrate	/Oisosuna (Sea gravel), Power Sand L, Bacter 100, Clear Super
CO_2	/Pollen Glass Beetle 50 x 4 units, 5 bubbles per second via CO_2 Beetle Counter x 4 units
Aeration	/14 hours after the light is turned off using Pollen Glass Beetle 50 for AIR x 2 units with NA Control Timer
Additives	/Brighty K; Green Brighty STEP 1
Water Change	/1/2 once a week
Water Quality	/Temperature 77°F; pH 7.0; TH 20mg/l
Aquatic Plants	/*Riccia fluitans*
	Eleocharis acicularis
Animals	/*Paracheirodon axelrodi*
	Caridina japonica
	Otocinclus sp.

My Philosophy for Iwagumi

A rock does not allow for compromise or fudging because of its strength and presence. This is one reason why creating an Iwagumi layout is considered difficult. Indeed, I had to rearrange rocks many times in the past before I finished an Iwagumi layout. It took me a long time before I acquired my own sense for rock arrangement. A rock is a mirror-like material that reflects the creator's intension very clearly. A landscaper, Enshu Kobori (1579—1647) is said to have perfected his rock arranging method through sketching many oceans and mountain streams. This great artist must have learned rock arrangements through studying streams in nature. I consider looking at nature and art work in other fields and developing one's own point of view as the best method for developing the rock arrangement skill, rather than studying other people's Iwagumi layouts.

My own philosophy for Iwagumi progressed in three stages. It progressed just as my idea about how a landscape gardener's method of work changed. At first, I admired the landscape gardeners who took time to plan and thought things through. Then, I came to think that a landscape gardener's experience and senses were reflected in the speed of his work. Lastly, I've come to consider the difference between working quickly with an understanding of what you're working with and getting the work done without thinking anything.

Throwing something together quickly is different from being able to make one's own judgment at once. If you are not experienced at creating layouts, making a lot of attempts and gaining experience from them often results in a better layout. Especially in the case of an Iwagumi layout, you should rearrange rocks hundreds of times over the substrate until you can come up with a satisfactory result. Such efforts always pay off later as one's experience.

TAKASHI AMANO

NATURE AQUARIUM

COMPLETE WORKS

1997-1999

DATA

Date	January, 1997
Aquarium	W71 x D39 x H35 (in)
Lighting	NA Lamp 40W x 4 units, NA Lamp 20W x 14 units, turned on for 10 hours
Filter	External Filter, Bio Rio
Substrate	Oisosuna (Sea gravel), Power Sand L, Bacter 100, Clear Super
CO_2	Pollen Glass Beetle 50 x 2 units, 5 bubbles per second via CO_2 Beetle Counter x 2 units
Aeration	14 hours after the light is turned off using Pollen Glass Beetle 50 for AIR with NA Control Timer
Additives	Brighty K; Green Brighty Special LIGHTS; ECA
Water Change	1/3 once a week
Water Quality	Temperature 79°F; pH 6.8; TH 20mg/l
Aquatic Plants	*Riccia fluitans*
	Eleocharis acicularis
	Fontinalis antipyretica
	Anubias barteri var. *nana*
	Hemianthus micranthemoides var.
	Ludwigia incrinata
	Ludwigia arcuata
	Nymphaea sp.
	Nymphaea sp.
	Nymphaea rubra
Animals	*Paracheirodon axelrodi*
	Thayeria boehlkei
	Nematobrycon palmeri
	Moenkhausia pittieri
	Hyphessobrycon erythrostigma
	Iguanodectes spilurus
	Thoracocharax stellatus
	Otocinclus sp.
	Caridina japonica

Stem Plants in a Large Aquarium

Stem plants have been popular as plants for an aquarium for many years since they come in many varieties and are easy to obtain. However, back when a CO_2 injection system and a bright lighting fixture were not yet available, these plants looked very different from the way they grew in nature. The stems of stem plants grew very spindly toward the water surface, and the sections between nodes were elongated as well. These conditions did not improve much and I always felt something was not right in those days.

Then one day when I was taking underwater photographs in the ocean near Sado Island, I happened to notice that the red part of my jacket appeared very dark while the blue part appeared just like the original blue color. As I looked aside, I saw that seagrass *Zostera marina* was photosynthesizing vigorously, producing a lot of air bubbles under such a condition. The thought that plants may be using blue spectrum to photosynthesize underwater crossed my mind. The lamp that was commonly used for growing aquatic plants was the same grow light for gardening, used for growing

terrestrial plants. Therefore, it produced primarily the red spectrum of light that terrestrial plants use to photosynthesize.

The development of NA (metal halide) lamp changed the way that aquatic plants grew dramatically. The sections between nodes became shorter and the density of leaves increased, allowing stem plants to form bushes. Consequently, it became possible to maintain them through trimming. Until that time, stem plants were maintained by uprooting them, cutting their upper sections to an even length, and then replanting the evenly cut sections. Instead, the tops of stem plants develop multiple new shoots through trimming. Terminal buds grow densely and evenly through repeated trimming, and eventually a stem plant forms a beautiful bush. The innovative method of expression was developed with the use of rosette plants and composition materials in the middle ground to hide the unsightly individual stems below the initial cut surfaces. Since the blue light contained in an NA lamp reaches the deeper area of an aquarium, the growth of underbrush improved as well.

It also became possible to grow stem plants in a larger, deeper aquarium by providing adequately bright light through placing enough NA lamps to cover the top of the aquarium. The large space allowed stem plants to develop into larger bushes and appear more natural. Stem plants spread their branches in a bright water column and develop dense leaves in nature. Although viewers may associate their appearance with manicured shrubbery in a garden, this is actually how stem plants look naturally.

DATA

		Aquatic Plants	/Glossostigma elatinoides
Date	/March, 1997		
Aquarium	/W35 x D18 x H18 (in)		Riccia fluitans
Lighting	/NA Lamp 32W x 6 units, turned on for 10 hours		Eleocharis acicularis
Filter	/External Filter, Bio Rio, Bamboo Charcoal, Palm Net		Cyperus helferi
Substrate	/Aqua Soil Amazonia, Power Sand M, Bacter 100, Clear Super		Isoetes japonica
CO₂	/Pollen Glass Beetle 40, 3 bubbles per second via CO₂ Beetle Counter	Animals	/Paracheirodon axelrodi
			Caridina japonica
Aeration	/14 hours after the light is turned off using Pollen Glass Beetle 40 for AIR with NA Control Timer		Otocinclus sp.
Additives	/Brighty K; Green Brighty Special LIGHTS; Phyton Git		
Water Change	/1/3 once a week		
Water Quality	/Temperature 79°F; pH 6.8; TH 50mg/l		

DATA

		Aquatic Plants	/ *Glossostigma elatinoides*
Date	/ April, 1997		*Riccia fluitans*
Aquarium	/ W47 x D18 x H18 (in)		*Eleocharis acicularis*
Lighting	/ NA Lamp 20W x 12 units, turned on for 10 hours	Animals	/ *Paracheirodon simulans*
Filter	/ External Filter, Bio Rio, Bamboo Charcoal, Palm Net		*Caridina japonica*
Substrate	/ Aqua Soil Malaya, Power Sand M, Bacter 100, Clear Super		*Otocinclus* sp.
CO₂	/ Pollen Glass Beetle 50, 3 bubbles per second via CO₂ Beetle Counter		
Aeration	/ 14 hours after the light is turned off using Pollen Glass Beetle 50 for AIR with NA Control Timer		
Additives	/ Brighty K; Green Brighty Special LIGHTS; Green Bacter		
Water Change	/ 1/3 once a week		
Water Quality	/ Temperature 77°F; pH 7.0; TH 20mg/l		

DATA

Date	/June, 1997	Aquatic Plants/	*Riccia fluitans*
Aquarium	/W71 x D24 x H24 (in)		*Eleocharis acicularis*
Lighting	/NA Lamp 20W x 24 units, turned on for 10 hours		*Rotala wallichii*
Filter	/External Filter, Bio Rio, Bamboo Charcoal, Palm Net		*Rotala rotundifolia*
Substrate	/Aqua Soil Amazonia, Power Sand L, Bacter 100,		*Rotala macrandra*
	Clear Super, Penac W for aquarium, Penac P		*Rotala rotundifolia* (green)
CO₂	/Pollen Glass Beetle 50 x 2 units, 3 bubbles per second		*Micranthemum unbrosum*
	via CO₂ Beetle Counter x 2 units		*Ludwigia ovaris*
Aeration	/14 hours after the light is turned off using Pollen		*Ludwigia perennsis*
	Glass Beetle 50 for AIR with NA Control Timer		*Polygonum* sp. "pink"
Additives	/Brighty K; ECA	Animals/	*Paracheirodon axelrodi*
Water Change	/1/3 twice a week		*Caridina japonica*
Water Quality	/Temperature 77°F; pH 6.0; TH 50mg/l		*Otocinclus* sp.

Water Purification by Aquatic Plants

One of the benefits of growing fish and aquatic plants together besides the aesthetic value is the ability of aquatic plants to purify water. Aquatic plants absorb carbon dioxide exhaled by fishes, and they release a large amount of oxygen through photosynthesis. Uneaten food and wastes that are decomposed by bacteria are used by aquatic plants as nutrients. The nutrient uptake and secondary oxygenation through photosynthesis are not the only water purification effects of aquatic plants. Aquatic plants are grown densely in Nature Aquarium, and the dense, healthy growth of aquatic plants also suppresses the development of blue green algae. Algae not only trouble aquarists but also aquatic plants as well, for algae are the natural enemy of the plants and

threaten their lives. When aquatic plants are growing well, they are thought to produce some substances that suppress the development of algae.

Aquatic plants that grow near the waterfront, such as reeds, have maintained the good water quality of lakes and rivers where they grow. However, the vegetation at water's edges disappeared due to concrete revetment and repair works, and the destruction of the ecosystem and eutrophication resulting from human sewage contamination ensued. Even in the isolated ecosystem of an aquarium, overly abundant nitrogenous materials are produced from dead leaves, uneaten food, and fish waste. When they become excessive, aquatic plants cannot keep up with them, and algae will gradually take over the aquarium. The ecosystem inside

the aquarium will suffer from a terminal condition and the aquascape may even be destroyed. Preventing the generation of a eutrophic environment is the countermeasure, as in the case of global environment. Therefore, the only fertilizers that can be added to an aquarium should be trace elements such as potassium, iron, manganese, and silicon, which cannot be produced inside an aquarium. Heliophytes, such as *Riccia* and stem plants in particular, grow fast and absorb nutrients actively. It is necessary to fertilize based on the characteristic, volume, and condition of aquatic plants. We are learning about ecosystems in a practical manner through material cycling and by maintaining the balance of fauna and flora.

DATA

Date	June, 1997	Aquatic Plants	*Cryptocoryne beckettii*
Aquarium	W35 x D18 x H18 (in)		*Cryptocoryne willisii*
Lighting	NA Lamp 32W x 6 units, turned on for 10 hours		*Cryptocoryne parva*
Filter	External Filter, Bio Rio, Bamboo Charcoal		*Cryptocoryne wendtii (Tropica)*
Substrate	Aqua Soil Malaya, Power Sand Special M, Bacter 100,		*Cryptocoryne undulata*
	Clear Super, Penac W for aquarium, Penac P		*Cryptocoryne balansae*
CO₂	Pollen Glass Beetle 40, 3 bubbles per second via CO₂	Animals	*Trigonostigma heteromorpha*
	Beetle Counter		*Caridina japonica*
Aeration	14 hours after the light is turned off using Pollen		*Otocinclus* **sp.**
	Glass Beetle 30 for AIR with NA Control Timer		
Additives	Brighty K; Green Brighty Special SHADE; ECA		
Water Change	1/3 one every three days		
Water Quality	Temperature 77°F; pH 6.8; TH 50mg/l		

DATA

Date	September, 1997
Aquarium	W24 x D12 x H14 (in)
Lighting	NA Lamp 20W x 4 units, turned on for 10 hours
Filter	External Filter, Bio Rio, NA Carbon, Palm Net
Substrate	Aqua Soil Mayala, Power Sand Special S, Bacter 100, Clear Super, Penac W for Aquarium, Penac P
CO$_2$	Pollen Glass, 2 bubbles per second via CO$_2$ Bubble Counter
Aeration	14 hours after the light is turned off using Pollen Glass for AIR with NA Control Timer
Additives	Brighty K; Green Brighty Special SHADE
Water Change	1/3 twice a week
Water Quality	Temperature 77°F; pH 7.0; TH 50mg/l
Aquatic Plants	*Cryptocoryne willisii*
	Cryptocoryne parva
	Cryptocoryne tonkinensis
Animals	*Rasbora sarawakensis*
	Caridina japonica
	Otocinclus sp.

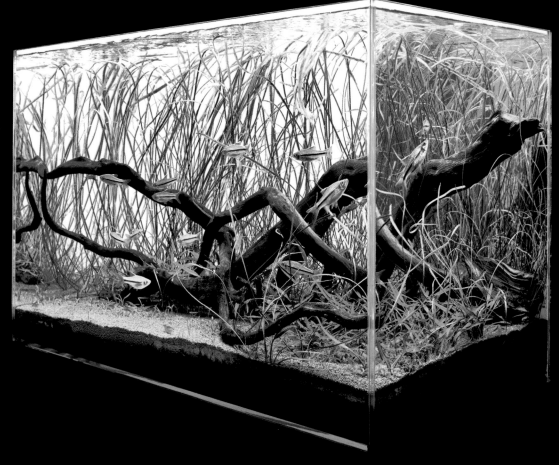

DATA

Date	April, 1997
Aquarium	W24 x D12 x H14 (in)
Lighting	NA Lamp 20W x 4 units, turned on for 10 hours
Filter	External Filter, Bio Rio, Bamboo Charcoal, Palm Net
Substrate	Aqua Soil Amazonia, Power Sand S, Bacter 100, Clear Super
CO$_2$	Pollen Glass, 3 bubbles per second via CO$_2$ Bubble Counter
Aeration	14 hours after the light is turned off using Pollen Glass for AIR with NA Control Timer
Additives	Brighty K; ECA; Phyton Git
Water Change	1/3 once a week
Water Quality	Temperature 77°F; pH 7.0; TH 20mg/l
Aquatic Plants	*Glossostigma elatinoides*
	Eleocharis acicularis
	Riccia fluitans
	Eleocharis vivipara
Animals	*Hemigrammus hyanuary*
	Caridina japonica
	Otocinclus sp.

DATA

Date	/June, 1997	Aquatic Plants	/*Cryptocoryne balansae*
Aquarium	/W138 x D29.5 x H29.5 (in)		*Cryptocoryne retrospiralis*
Lighting	/NA Lamp 40W x 8 units; 20W x 4 units, turned on for 10 hours		*Cryptocoryne lucens*
Filter	/External Filter, Bio Rio		*Cryptocoryne parva*
Substrate	/Aqua Soil Amazonia, Power Sand Special L, Bacter 100, Clear Super, Penac W for Aquarium, Penac P		*Cryptocoryne costata*
			Marcilea crenata
CO₂	/Pollen Glass Beetle 50 x 4 units, 3 bubbles per second via CO₂ Beetle Counter x 4 units		*Fontinalis antipyretica*
		Animals	/*Rasboroides vaterifloris*
Aeration	/14 hours after the light is turned off using Pollen Glass Beetle 50 for AIR x 2 units with NA Control Timer		*Rasbora caudimaculata*
			Danio malabaricus
Additives	/Brighty K; ECA		*Trichogaster leeri*
Water Change	/1/3 once a week		*Caridina japonica*
Water Quality	/Temperature 77°|F; pH 6.8; TH 50mg/l		*Otocinclus* sp.

A Layout That Takes the Changes Over Time into Consideration
Aquariums that are set up in stores and public places on maintenance contracts need to be created by taking into consideration changes that will occur over time, since their layouts cannot be revamped frequently. I base my design decisions with the idea of maintaining it for at least 10 years. Some plants, such as stem plants, grow well while the substrate is relatively new but do poorly as the substrate ages. On the other hand, some plants like *Cryptocoryne* grow better when the substrate matures to some extent. I arrange these plants so that a layout will undergo transitions gradually from one to the other. Especially in the case of an aquarium on a maintenance contract, aquatic plants need to be arranged by taking into consideration the changing power relationships of the plants from the beginning.

In the case of an aquarium that is not on a maintenance contract, I often create a layout considering the ease of maintenance rather than changes that will occur over time. I had an opportunity to have a close talk with a group of leading Japanese garden landscapers some years ago. One of the subjects that came up in the meeting was the difficult problem that they were faced with, which was the fact that there was a shortage of people who would take over and maintain finished gardens, though there were many garden landscapers who designed and built gardens. They voiced their serious concerns that there would be a huge problem in the future if we continued to design and build gardens mindlessly without training people who could take over and maintain them. The same thing is true with Nature Aquarium, in which daily maintenance is naturally very important.

I am good at creating layouts but not very fond of the work required to maintain them. Maintenance work has its own challenges, and it requires organization and determination. Therefore, my works are created with provisions for the people who maintain them. Although I create a layout, the layout cannot be maintained for a long period of time unless it is a type of layout that everybody can maintain. A layout that appears complex like nature at a glance but is still easy to maintain is the type of layout that I strive to produce. No matter how intricate and refined, if a layout takes a lot of work to maintain it, Nature Aquarium will never grow out of the realm of minority. I believe that proposing a type of layout that ordinary people can maintain for a long time on their own is the key for Nature Aquarium to become more widespread.

DATA

Date	November, 1997
Aquarium	W47 x D18 x H18 (in)
Lighting	NA Lamp 20W x 12 units, turned on for 10 hours
Filter	External Filter, Bio Cube 20, NA Carbon
Substrate	Aqua Soil Africana, Power Sand M, Bacter 100, Clear Super
CO_2	Pollen Glass Beetle 50, 3 bubbles per second via CO_2 Beetle Counter
Aeration	14 hours after the light is turned off using Lily Pipe P-6
Additives	Brighty K; ECA
Water Change	1/3 twice a week
Water Quality	Temperature 77°F; pH 6.8; TH 10mg/l
Aquatic Plants	**Willow Moss from Malaysia**
	Willow Moss from Taiwan
Animals	*Ladigesia roloffi*
	Otocinclus **sp.**
	Caridina japonica

DATA

Date	December, 1997
Aquarium	W35 x D18 x H18 (in)
Lighting	NA Lamp 32W x 6 units, turned on for 10 hours
Filter	External Filter, Bio Rio, NA Carbon
Substrate	Aqua Soil Malaya, Power Sand M, Bacter 100, Clear Super, Penac W for Aquarium, Penac P
CO$_2$	Pollen Glass Beetle 50, 4 bubbles per second via CO$_2$ Beetle Counter
Aeration	14 hours after the light is turned off using Pollen Glass Beetle 50 for AIR
Additives	Brighty K; Green Brighty STEP 1
Water Change	1/4 twice a week
Water Quality	Temperature 77°F; pH 6.8; TH 20mg/l
Aquatic Plants	*Bolbitis heudelotii*
	Ludwigia arcuata
	Microsorum pteropus
	Glossostigma elatinoides
	Riccia fluitans
	Fontinalis antipyretica
Animals	*Hemiodopsis sterni*
	Gasteropelecus sternicla
	Hyphessobrycon columbianus
	Caridina japonica
	Otocinclus **sp.**

DATA

Date	╱October, 1998
Aquarium	╱W35 x D18 x H18 (in)
Lighting	╱NA Lamp 32W x 6 units, turned on for 10 hours
Filter	╱External Filter, Bio Cube 20, NA Carbon
Substrate	╱Aqua Soil Amazonia, Power Sand M, Bacter 100, Clear Super, Penac W for Aquarium, Penac P
CO₂	╱Pollen Glass Beetle 40, 3 bubbles per second via CO_2 Beetle Counter
Aeration	╱14 hours after the light is turned off using Lily Pipe P-4
Additives	╱Brighty K; Green Brighty STEP 1
Water Change	╱1/3 once a week
Water Quality	╱Temperature 77ºF; pH 6.8; TH 50mg/l

Aquatic Plants	╱*Microsorum* sp.
	Polygonum sp."pink"
	Echinodorus tenellus
Animals	╱*Hyphessobrycon sweglesi*
	Crossocheilus siamensis
	Caridina japonica
	Otocinclus sp.

DATA

Date	/June, 1998
Aquarium	/W35 x D18 x H24 (in)
Lighting	/NA Lamp 32W x 6 units, turned on for 10 hours
Filter	/External Filter, Bio Rio, NA Carbon
Substrate	/Aqua Soil Amazonia, Power Sand M, Bacter 100, Clear Super, Penac W for Aquarium, Penac P
CO₂	/Pollen Glass Beetle 40, 3 bubbles per second via CO₂ Beetle Counter
Aeration	/14 hours after the light is turned off using Pollen Glass Beetle 40 for AIR
Additives	/Brighty K; Green Brighty STEP 1
Water Change	/1/3 once a week
Water Quality	/Temperature 77°F; pH 6.8; TH 10mg/l

Aquatic Plants	/*Fontinalis antipyretica*
	Riccia fluitans
	Microsorum sp.
	Hygrophila stricta
Animals	/*Rasbora kalochroma*
	Caridina japonica
	Otocinclus sp.

1 : An ideal substrate environment is one in which roots of aquatic plants and various microorganisms can cohabitate. It is especially important that microorganisms are working actively there. To ensure this, Bacter 100, which contains more than 100 different types of dormant microorganisms, is scattered evenly over the bottom of an aquarium. Since it contains a variety of microorganisms instead of a few specific types, a microbiota suitable for each aquarium environment will be established. Then Clear Super, a food for microorganisms that encourages them to multiply, is scattered in the same manner. Microorganisms develop and multiply within the substrate with the synergistic effect of the two products.

2 : Power Sand is the foundation of the substrate. An appropriate amount of product, which comes three sizes, S, M, and L, should be used depending on the water depth of the aquarium being used. In th case of the 35 x 18 x 18 inch aquarium in this picture, three bags of Power Sand M (2 liters) were use Since pumice, the base material of Power Sand, is porous and highly water permeable, it prevents har ening in the lowest part of the substrate, which constitutes the point of weakness for an aquarium. I plant-based, organic nutrients encourage microorganisms to multiply. The slow-release nutrients provic nutrition to plant roots over a long period of time and develop a living substrate system.

*Steps 1 and 2 above can be performed in reverse ord

5: Driftwood pieces were arranged further to establish space in the center of the U-shaped composition, watching the left and right balance of the layout. The angle of the line formed by the driftwood in this step is important. The layout appears unnatural if the line is too straight or if some elements in the two groups produce parallel lines. Since there were some extra spaces at both ends of the aquarium after the driftwood was arranged, I decided to stack some stones to which willow moss was attached with Moss Cotton. By the time willow moss grows and attaches itself to the stones, driftwood and rocks will blend well and the middle ground will be formed naturally. This completes the framework of the composition.

6: Planting of aquatic plants comes next. As a basic rule, just enough water is added to the aquarium submerge the substrate as shown in the picture, and then planting work starts with underbrush plant The planting work progresses toward the background, and the water level is gradually increased as th work progresses. Working in this manner not only reduces the buoyancy of the aquatic plants and make it easier to plant, but it also keeps hands from getting wet. Cobra grass, which is used in this layou should be planted densely, using tweezers designed for planting aquatic plants, since it develops on one leaf at a time and therefore takes a long time to grow densely.

: Next, three bags of Aqua Soil Amazonia (2.5 gallons), rich in humus and effective for growing aquatic lants, were laid to the thickness shown in the picture. When creating a layout with driftwood, sloping he material from the foreground toward the background enhances the sense of depth. Then, the ubstrate level was adjusted, watching the thickness of the foreground since it can appear overpowering laid too thick. Applying powder-type Aqua Soil thinly over the surface as a finishing material improves e appearance of the substrate and makes it easier to plant aquatic plants.

4: Driftwood comprises the framework of a composition. The overall direction of a layout is set by how driftwood is arranged. Old black wood is arranged in a U-shaped composition in this layout. If the driftwood's surface appears too dark or if its shape is not good, willow moss should be attached to it Doing so increases the natural feel of the layout and it helps create an aquascape that allows its viewers to sense the passage of time. First, the two main driftwood pieces were placed in the left and right sides of the aquarium. The area in front of the driftwood became the foreground and the area behind it became the background, thereby establishing the ratio of planting spaces.

After the underbrush plants are planted, the water level is increased enough to submerge the back- ound area of the substrate, and aquatic plants for the background are planted. A planting scheme to eate an empty space in the center of the U-shaped composition is used here. Low growing *Blyxa* "short af" was used in the center of this layout, and *Blyxa aubertii*, which is in the same *Blyxa* family but grows ller, were selected for the left and right sides of the *Blyxa* "short leaf". Since these plants alone cannot eate enough of a sense of depth, rhizomes of *Bolbitis* were attached with Wood Tight to various parts of

8: After all the aquatic plants were planted, tap water was added gradually. Since tap water contains residual chlorine that is toxic to living organisms, a dechlorinator, such as Chlor-Off, was used to detoxify the chlorine. Since Aqua Soil contains a large amount of natural soil-based organic nutrients, the water tends to turn cloudy during the initial setup period. Therefore, water changes are performed as frequently as possible only during the initial setup period to eliminate the excess organic nutrients. CO_2 injection was started at the rate of one bubble per second using a CO_2 Beetle Counter, and the rate was gradually

DATA

Date	October, 1998
Aquarium	W35 x D18 x H18 (in)
Lighting	NA Lamp 32W x 6 units, turned on for 10 hours
Filter	Super Jet Filter ES-600, Bio Cube 20, NA Carbon, Palm Net
Substrate	Aqua Soil Amazonia, Power Sand M, Bacter 100, Clear Super, Penac W for Aquarium, Penac P
CO_2	Pollen Glass Beetle 40, 3 bubbles per second via CO_2 Beetle Counter
Aeration	14 hours after the light is turned off using Pollen Glass Beetle 40 for AIR with NA Control Timer
Additives	Brighty K; ECA
Water Change	1/3 once a week
Water Quality	Temperature 77°F; pH 6.6; TH 20mg/l
Aquatic Plants	*Lilaeopsis novae-zelandiae*
	Blyxa japonica
	Blyxa auberti
	Bolbitis heudelotii
	Fontinalis antipyretica
Animals	*Rasbora kalochroma*
	Rasbora vaterifloris
	Trigonostigma heteromorpha
	Otocinclus sp.
	Crossocheilus siamensis
	Caridina japonica

DATA

Date	October, 1998
Aquarium	W71 x D24 x H24 (in)
Lighting	NA Lamp 20W x 24 units, turned on for 10 hours
Filter	External Filter, Bio Cube 20, NA Carbon
Substrate	Aqua Soil Amazonia, Power Sand L, Bacter 100,
	Clear Super, Penac W for Aquarium, Penac P
CO₂	Pollen Glass Beetle 50, 5 bubbles per second via CO₂
	Beetle Counter
Aeration	14 hours after the light is turned off using Lily Pipe P-6
Additives	Brighty K; Green Brighty STEP 2
Water Change	1/3 once a week
Water Quality	Temperature 77°F; pH 6.8; TH 50mg/l
Aquatic Plants	*Bolbitis heudelotii*
	Lilaeopsis brasiliensis
	Cryptocoryne wendtii
	Cryptocoryne costata
	Cryptocoryne sp.
	Hygrophila angustifolia
	Hygrophila stricta
Animals	*Rasbora kalochroma*
	Trigonostigma heteromorpha
	Rasbora trilineata
	Otocinclus sp.
	Caridina japonica

DATA

Date	March, 1998
Aquarium	W47 x D39 x H29.5 (in)
Lighting	NA Lamp 20W x 20 units, turned on for 10 hours
Filter	External Filter, Bio Rio, NA Carbon
Substrate	Aqua Soil Malaya, Power Sand Special L, Bacter 100, Clear Super, Penac W for Aquarium, Penac P
CO₂	Pollen Glass Beetle 50 x 2 units, 3 bubbles per second via CO₂ Beetle Counter x 2 units
Aeration	14 hours after the light is turned off using Pollen Glass Beetle 50 for AIR
Additives	Brighty K; ECA
Water Change	1/3 twice a week
Water Quality	Temperature 77°F; pH 6.8; TH 20mg/l
Aquatic Plants	*Anubias barteri* var. *nana*
	Bolbitis heudelotii
	Fontinalis antipyretica
	Aponogeton rigidifolius
Animals	*Phenacogrammus interruptus*
	Arnoldichthys spilopterus
	Otocinclus sp.
	Caridina japonica

DATA

Date	/September, 1998	Aquatic Plants	/Glossostigma elatinoides
Aquarium	/W94.5 x D24 x H24 (in)		Riccia fluitans
Lighting	/110W x 4 units, turned on for 10 hours		Fontinalis antipyretica
Filter	/External Filter, Bio Rio, NA Carbon		Echinodorus uruguaiensis
Substrate	/Aqua Soil Amazonia, Power Sand L, Bacter 100,		Echinodorus latifolius
	Clear Super, Penac W for Aquarium, Penac P		Echinodorus major
CO₂	/Pollen Glass Beetle 50 x 2 units, 3 bubbles per second		Echinodorus sp. "Rubin" (narrow leaf)
	via CO₂ Beetle Counter x 2 units		Echinodorus sp. "ozelot"
Aeration	/14 hours after the light is turned off using Pollen Glass		Hygrophila lacustris
	Beetle 50 for AIR with NA Control Timer		Blyxa auberti
Additives	/Brighty K; Green Gain; Green Brighty Special LIGHTS; ECA		Cyperus helferi
Water Change	/1/4 once a week		Crinum natans
Water Quality	/Temperature 77°F; pH 6.8; TH 20mg/l		Hygrophila sp.
		Animals	/Melanotaenia praecox
			Crossocheilus siamensis
			Caridina japonica
			Otocinclus sp.

The Celebration of Analog

If an electric appliance breaks, it is often quicker and cheaper to replace it than to fix it. The concept of repairing things cannot keep up with a modern world that keeps on advancing and changing. With the upsurge of factories, all of us can obtain good products inexpensively through mass production, but we have gotten used to throwing things away. Are we losing our conscience to take good care of things?

One of my hobbies is collecting analog tools, such as fountain pens, microscopes, Leica and other old wood cameras, and gramophones. When I handle a tool that someone created care-fully with his soul, it gives me the satisfaction of using a well-crafted tool. One can develop an attachment to a well-crafted tool as one uses it. It is often passed down as an heirloom to the next generation. Before the time of mass-production by machines, people took care of things with affection, and it was common to have usable items passed down. As a tradeoff for a highly developed consumer society, nature is disappearing around us and the world is overflowing with materials that are turning into a large amount of garbage. The garbage has nowhere to go and this brings further destruction of nature.

Facing this current situation, I believe that the role of ADA as a manufacturer is to maintain our insistence on quality and to provide a good product that can be used for a long time. Although a handcrafted product can only be produced in a limited number at a time, it is produced with the soul of its creator. One's affection for a fine material is like a window of the soul that reflects one's affection for nature. One's insistence on and affection for finer things are connected deep down with the origin of Nature Aquarium, which is based on the idea that "One who cannot love her smallest creations, cannot claim to stand before nature."

DATA
Date   May, 1999
Aquarium   W47 x D18 x H24 (in)
Lighting   NA Lamp 20W x 12 units, turned on for 10 hours
Filter   Super Jet Filter ES-1200, Bio Rio
Substrate   Aqua Soil Amazonia, Power Sand Special L, Bacter 100,
              Clear Super, Penac W for Aquarium, Penac P
CO₂   Pollen Glass Beetle 50, 4 bubbles per second via CO₂
              Beetle Counter
Aeration   14 hours after the light is turned off using Lily Pipe P-6
Additives   Brighty K; Green Brighty STEP 1
Water Change 1/3 once a week
Water Quality Temperature 77°F; pH 6.4; TH 20mg/l
Aquatic Plants *Lilaeopsis brasiliensis*
              Eleocharis acicularis
              Eleocharis vivipara
Animals   *Iguanodectes spilurus*
              Crossocheilus siamensis
              Caridina japonica
              Otocinclus sp.

DATA

Date	/ March, 1999
Aquarium	/ W138 x D29.5 x H29.5 (in)
Lighting	/ NA Lamp 20W x 32 units, NA Lamp 40W x 5 units, turned on for 10 hours
Filter	/ External Filter, Bio Rio, NA Carbon
Substrate	/ Aqua Soil Amazonia, Power Sand Special L, Bacter 100,
	Clear Super, Penac W for Aquarium, Penac P
CO_2	/ Pollen Glass Beetle 50 x 4 units, 4 bubbles per second via CO_2 Beetle
	Counter x 4 units
Aeration	/ 14 hours after the light is turned off using Pollen Glass Beetle 50 for AIR
	with NA Control Timer
Additives	/ Brighty K; Green Brighty STEP 1
Water Change	/ 1/4 once a week
Water Quality	/ Temperature 77°F; pH 7.0; TH 20mg/l
Aquatic Plants	/ *Eleocharis acicularis*
	Eleocharis vivipara
	Riccia fluitans
Animals	/ *Paracheirodon axelrodi*
	Crossocheilus siamensis
	Caridina japonica

Quintessence of Iwagumi

Although there are many cerebrated gardens in Kyoto, there isn't a rock garden that seems to be built with the dynamics of water movement in mind. It may be due to the fact that the creators are not concerned with a constant water flow, but the rock placement is unnatural and there is no relevance between the rocks and other elements. The sizes of the rocks are appropriate and their placements are well balanced, but the rocks are not placed naturally and attractively in the patterns of the water flow drawn on the sand. Although the placement is often said to replicate nature, the rock arrangement does not make sense from such a point of view. It sounds like an explanation that was attached later. However, it is my opinion that we find it relaxing to stand in front of such a rock garden because it makes us aware of the

great passage of time since the Muromachi era (1336-1467). It may also be because the borrowed scenery from the surrounding landscape and the overall atmosphere of the place that surrounds the rock garden make up for the inadequacy of the rock placement.

When I create an Iwagumi layout for Nature Aquarium, I am conscious of water flow and think a great deal of how things appear in nature. Having taken many photographs of rivers and oceans of the Amazon, Africa, Borneo, and Japan, every rocky landscape that I saw has been stored unconsciously in my mind. They sharpen my sensitivity and give me the energy to recreate them in an aquarium. If I had more rocks, I could create a greater variety of Iwagumi layouts, but unfortunately I am too busy to collect rocks at leisure.

An Iwagumi layout is well recognized in the world and has gained quite a lot of popularity among aquatic plant layout enthusiasts. However, a lot of layouts seem to be at the mercy of the rocks themselves, and the originality of the creators seem to be somewhat obscured. My true sentiment is that an Iwagumi layout cannot be created without knowing rocks first. It is best to go to where rocks exist to find out about rocks. How do they look in mountain streams or in the ocean? One can only draw so much for ideas out of books and photographs or one's own image of rocks. The hint for maintaining an aquarium where one can keep fish easily and that is soothing to oneself at the same time is hidden in nature where rocks were born.

DATA
Date   May, 1999
Aquarium   W35 x D18 x H18 (in)
Lighting   NA Lamp 32W x 6 units, turned on for 10 hours
Filter   Super Jet Filter ES-600, Bio Cube 20, Anthracite
Substrate   Aqua Soil Amazonia, Power Sand M, Bacter 100,
                Clear Super, Penac W for Aquarium, Penac P
CO₂   Pollen Glass Beetle 40, 3 bubbles per second via CO₂
                Beetle Counter
Aeration   14 hours after the light is turned off using Lily Pipe P-4
Additives   Brighty K; Green Brighty STEP 1
Water Change   1/3 once a week
Water Quality   Temperature 77°F; pH 6.0; TH 20mg/l

Aquatic Plants *Eleocharis acicularis*
Animals   *Paracheirodon simulans*
                Crossocheilus siamensis
                Caridina japonica
                Otocinclus sp.

DATA

Date	September, 1998
Aquarium	W24 x D12 x H14 (in)
Lighting	NA Lamp 20W x 4 units, turned on for 10 hours
Filter	Super Jet Filter ES-600, Bio Cube 20, Anthracite
Substrate	Aqua Soil Amazonia, Power Sand S, Bacter 100, Clear Super, Penac W for Aquarium, Penac P
CO₂	Pollen Glass Large 20, 2 bubbles per second via CO₂ Bubble Counter
Aeration	14 hours after the light is turned off using Pollen Glass Large 20 for AIR with NA Control Timer
Additives	Brighty K; Green Brighty STEP 1; ECA
Water Change	1/3 once a week
Water Quality	Temperature 77°F; pH 7.2; TH 50mg/l
Aquatic Plants	*Marsilea crenata*
	Lilaeopsis novae-zelandiae
	Eleocharis acicularis
	Echinodorus latifolius
Animals	*Hyphessobrycon amandae*
	Crossocheilus siamensis
	Otocinclus sp.
	Caridina japonica

DATA

Date	September, 1998
Aquarium	W35 x D18 x H18 (in)
Lighting	32W x 6 units, turned on for 10 hours
Filter	External Filter, Bio Cube 20, Palm Net, NA Carbon
Substrate	Aqua Soil Amazonia, Power Sand M, Bacter 100, Clear Super, Penac W for Aquarium, Penac P
CO₂	Pollen Glass Beetle 40, 3 bubbles per second via CO₂ Beetle Counter
Aeration	14 hours after the light is turned off using Pollen Glass Beetle 40 for AIR with NA Control Timer
Additives	Brighty K; ECA
Water Change	1/3 twice a week
Water Quality	Temperature 77°F; pH 6.4; TH 50mg/l
Aquatic Plants	*Eleocharis acicularis*
Animals	*Paracheirodon axelrodi*
	Crossocheilus siamensis
	Otocinclus sp.
	Caridina japonica

DATA

Date	╱November, 1999		*Rotala rotundifolia*
Aquarium	╱W47 x D18 x H18 (in)		*Rotala rotundifolia* (green)
Lighting	╱NA Lamp 20W x 12 units, turned on for 10 hours		*Hygrophila polysperma*
Filter	╱External Filter, Bio Rio, NA Carbon		*Bacopa caroliniana*
Substrate	╱Aqua Soil Amazonia, Rio Negro Sand, Power Sand M,		*Ludwigia glandulosa*
	Bacter 100, Clear Super, Penac W for Aquarium, Penac P		*Nymphaea micrantha*
CO₂	╱Pollen Glass Beetle 40, 4 bubbles per second via CO₂		*Anubias hastifolia*
	Beetle Counter		*Nymphaea* sp.
Aeration	╱14 hours after the light is turned off using Lily Pipe P-6		*Alternanthera reineckii*
Additives	╱Brighty K; Green Brighty STEP 1; ECA		*Rotala macrandra* sp.
Water Change	╱1/3 twice a week		*Heteranthera zosterifolia*
Water Quality	╱Temperature 77°F; pH 6.8; TH 20mg/l		*Eriocaulaceae* sp.
Aquatic Plants	╱*Riccia fluitans*		*Polygonum* sp."pink"
	Ludwigia repens		*Eusteralis stellata*
	Limnophila sessiliflora		*Hygrophila difformis*
	Ludwigia arcuata	Animals	╱*Hyphessobrycon sweglesi*
	Ludwigia sp.		*Nematobrycon lacortei*
	Eusteralis stellata		*Thoracocharax stellatus*
	Micranthemum unbrosum		*Nannobrycon eques*
	Hygrophila sp.		*Otocinclus* sp.
	Rotala nanjean		*Caridina japonica*

DATA

Date	November, 1999
Aquarium	W29.5 x D18 x H18 (in)
Lighting	NA Lamp 20W x 6 units, turned on for 10 hours
Filter	Super Jet Filter ES-600, Bio Cube 20, Anthracite
Substrate	Aqua Soil Amazonia, Power Sand M, Bacter 100, Clear Super, Penac W for Aquarium, Penac P
CO₂	Pollen Glass Beetle 30, 3 bubbles per second via CO₂ Beetle Counter
Aeration	14 hours after the light is turned off using Lily Pipe P-4
Additives	Brighty K; ECA
Water Change	1/3 once a week
Water Quality	Temperature 77°F; pH 6.8; TH 15mg/l
Aquatic Plants	*Marsilea crenata*
	Echinodorus tenellus
	Fontinalis antipyretica
	Hygrophila polysperma
	Rotala rotundifolia (green)
	Ludwigia sp.
	Ludwigia repens
Animals	*Trigonostigma espei*
	Puntius gerius
	Chela dadyburjori
	Otocinclus sp.
	Caridina japonica

The Criteria for Selecting Aquatic Plants for a Layout

I was already growing aquatic plants before I established the Nature Aquarium techniques contained in this photo book. I understood that thickets of aquatic plants existed where fish lived based on the childhood memory of catching fish in a lagoon. In the beginning, I was interested in tropical fishes. However, it looked unnatural to not have any aquatic plants in an aquarium and it made me feel uneasy. So I planted *Hygrophila polysperma* and Amazon sword, which were popular and easy to obtain in the early days. I tried various aquatic plants, one after another, as they became available in Japan. While doing so, I came to understand gradually how to grow aquatic plants, and my efforts gradually developed into an

aquatic plant layout. You may find it surprising, but aquatic plants were considered articles of consumption when I started growing aquatic plants. The idea was to replace a plant with a new one after one died. It was rather uncommon to cultivate them in an aquarium. Therefore, I had to come up with systems on my own to grow healthy aquatic plants, such as substrate, lighting, liquid fertilizers, and CO_2 injection systems.

As I grew better at growing aquatic plants, I started thinking about the way to present them. This led to today's Nature Aquarium style. The aquatic plants that are used in Nature Aquarium are basically those that grow well in an aquarium. However, there were many aquatic plants initially for which growing conditions

were not known. Although *Echinodorus tenellus* and *Glossostigma* are popular basic plants now, I learned to grow them only through trial and error, starting with plants in weak and questionable conditions. Although there are many plants that became quite popular in the course of time in the aquarium industry, I select plants for Nature Aquarium strictly based on the criteria that they go together well with a given layout. No matter how beautiful or rare a plant is by itself, I would not use it if it looks lost or odd in a layout. The harmony of an overall aquascape with fish swimming against the stage of aquatic plants results in the expression of a natural feeling.

DATA

Date	December, 1999
Aquarium	W47 x D18 x H18 (in)
Lighting	NA Lamp 20W x 12 units, turned on for 10 hours
Filter	External Filter, Bio Rio, NA Carbon
Substrate	Bright Sand, Power Sand M, Bacter 100, Clear Super, Penac W for Aquarium, Penac P
CO₂	Pollen Glass Beetle 50, 3 bubbles per second via CO₂ Beetle Counter
Aeration	14 hours after the light is turned off using Lily Pipe P-6
Additives	Brighty K; ECA
Water Change	1/4 once a week
Water Quality	Temperature 77°F; pH 6.8; TH 15mg/l
Aquatic Plants	*Eleocharis acicularis*
	Rotala rotundifolia (green)
	Rotala nanjean
	Micranthemum unbrosum
	Hemianthus micranthemoides
	Ludwigia arcuata
Animals	*Hemigrammus ulreyi*
	Otocinclus sp.
	Caridina japonica

DATA

Date	May, 1999
Aquarium	W35 x D18 x H18 (in)
Lighting	NA Lamp 32W x 6 units, turned on for 10 hours
Filter	Super Jet Filter ES-600, Bio Cube 20, NA Carbon
Substrate	Aqua Soil Amazonia, Power Sand M, Bacter 100, Clear Super, Penac W for Aquarium, Penac P
CO₂	Pollen Glass Beetle 40, 4 bubbles per second via CO₂ Beetle Counter
Aeration	14 hours after the light is turned off using Lily Pipe P-4
Additives	Brighty K; ECA
Water Change	1/4 once a week
Water Quality	Temperature 77°F; pH 6.0; TH 20mg/l
Aquatic Plants	*Riccia fluitans*
	Glossostigma elatinoides
	Rotala wallichii
	Rotala rotundifolia
	Rotala rotundifolia (green)
	Rotala macrandra sp.
	Ludwigia sp.
	Tonina sp.
	Polygonum sp."pink"
	Hygrophila sp.
	Micranthemum unbrosum
Animals	*Hemigrammus ocellifer*
	Hyphessobrycon haraldschultzi
	Thoracocharax stellatus
	Moenkhausia pittieri
	Hyphessobrycon sp.
	Otocinclus sp.
	Caridina japonica

TAKASHI AMANO
NATURE AQUARIUM
COMPLETE WORKS

2000-2004

DATA

Date	╱September, 2000
Aquarium	╱W71 x D24 x H24 (in)
Lighting	╱NA Lamp 20W x 24 units, turned on for 10 hours
Filter	╱Super Jet Filter ES-2400, Bio Rio
Substrate	╱Aqua Soil Amazonia, Power Sand Special L, Bacter 100, Clear Super, Penac W for Aquarium, Penac P
CO₂	╱Pollen Glass Beetle 50 x 2 units, 3 bubbles per second via CO₂ Beetle Counter x 2 units
Aeration	╱14 hours after the light is turned off using Pollen Glass Beetle 50 for AIR x 2 units
Additives	╱Brighty K; Green Brighty STEP 2; ECA
Water Change	╱1/2 once a week
Water Quality	╱Temperature 77°F; pH 6.8; TH 10mg/l

Aquatic Plants	╱*Eleocharis acicularis*
	Lilaeopsis novae-zelandiae
	Echinodorus tenellus
	Echinodorus angustifolia
	Eleocharis helferi
	Cryptocoryne balansae
Animals	╱*Hemigrammus ulreyi*
	Crossocheilus siamensis
	Otocinclus sp.
	Caridina japonica

DATA

Date	September, 2000
Aquarium	W35 x D18 x H18 (in)
Lighting	NA Lamp 32W x 6 units, turned on for 10 hours
Filter	Super Jet Filter ES-600, Bio Rio
Substrate	Bright Sand, Power Sand M, Bacter 100, Clear Super, Penac W for Aquarium, Penac P
CO₂	Pollen Glass Beetle 30, 3 bubbles per second via CO₂ Beetle Counter
Aeration	14 hours after the light is turned off using Lily Pipe P-4
Additives	Brighty K; Green Brighty STEP 1; ECA
Water Change	1/3 twice a week
Water Quality	Temperature 77°F; pH 7.0; TH 50mg/l

Aquatic Plants	*Eleocharis acicularis*
	Eleocharis vivipara
Animals	*Poecilia reticulata* var.
	Caridina japonica
	Otocinclus sp.

DATA
Date : September, 2000
Aquarium : W35 x D18 x H18 (in)
Lighting : NA Lamp 32W x 6 units, turned on for 10 hours
Filter : Super Jet Filter ES-1200, Bio Rio, NA Carbon
Substrate : Aqua Soil Amazonia, Power Sand Special L, Bacter 100, Clear Super, Penac W for Aquarium, Penac P
CO₂ : Pollen Glass Beetle 40, 4 bubbles per second via CO₂ Beetle Counter
Aeration : 14 hours after the light is turned off using Lily Pipe P-4
Additives : Brighty K; Green Brighty STEP 2; ECA
Water Change : 1/2 once a week
Water Quality : Temperature 77°F; pH 6.8; TH 20mg/l
Aquatic Plants : *Grossostigma elatinoides*
Echinodorus tenellus
Blyxa japonica
Hygrophila polysperma
Rotala rotundifolia (**green**)
Rotala rotundifolia
Animals : *Pterophyllum scalare*
Hyphessobrycon amapaensis
Gasteropelecus levis
Otocinclus **sp.**
Caridina japonica

DATA

Date / November, 2000

Aquarium / W71 x D24 x H24 (in)

Lighting / NA Lamp 20W x 24 units, turned on for 10 hours

Filte / External Filter, Bio Rio, NA Carbon

Substrate / Aqua Soil Amazonia, Nile Sand, Power Sand L ,Bacter 100, Clear Super, Penac W for Aquarium, Penac P

CO_2 / Pollen Glass Beetle 50 x 2 units, 3 bubbles per second via CO_2 Beetle Counter x 2 units

Aeration / 14 hours after the light is turned off using Pollen Glass Beetle 50 for AIR with NA Control Timer

Additives / Brighty K; Green Brighty STEP 1

Water Change / 1/4 once a week

Water Quality / Temperature 79°F; pH 7.0; TH 20mg/l

Aquatic Plants / *Vesicularia montagnei*
Eleocharis acicularis
Bolbitis heudelotii
Anubias barteri var. *nana*
Ottelia ulvifolia
Echinodorus bleheri
Cryptocoryne balansae

Crinum calamistratum
Cyperus helferi
Echinodorus angustifolia

Animals / *Pterophyllum altam*
Priapella intermedia
Hemigrammus erythrozonus
Gasteropelecus sternicla
Microgeophagus ramirezi
Hemigrammus ulreyi
Caridina japonica
Otocinclus sp.

A No Longer Familiar Nature

Far fewer children are said to be interested in keeping aquariums and other living things nowadays. Although this is supposedly the effect of cell phones and video games, this does not seem quite right to me. It seems to me that children are not interested in nature because there isn't any nature around them. Today's children grow up surrounded by computers and high tech home appliances, and this is because nature is no longer a familiar thing around the house from the time that they are born. People in my

age group who grew up playing in a natural environment are still interested in and are enjoying aquariums. I am afraid that today's children do not have many feelings toward nature. This seems to underscore the importance of childhood experiences. However, this is not the children's fault. Although some people take their children to resort areas in search of nature, taking them to such resort areas is pointless. What is important is to become familiar with nature in our day-to-day living. Nowadays, people see a bug in the house as an enemy. I feel that a house where even a bug does not show up is rather scary. I would like to live in an environment that attracts various living things. In the case of an aquatic plant layout, the ideal layout to me is one that fish find comfortable to live in. I create a layout keeping in mind the idea of a place that I would like to live in if I were a fish. Plants produce an environment of an old-growth forest where insects, birds, and small animals exist. Furthermore, the scenery of a place with a well-balanced ecosystem is beautiful. That is the healthy, natural state that I find extremely important. However, in reality, dams are built, new roads are cut, more and more animals are driven out of nature, and the ecosystem is getting distorted. I do not want to express an image of such a distorted ecosystem in an aquarium. Going to the old-growth forests of the Amazon, Africa, Yakushima Island, and Sado Island may be my escape from the current situation of living in the middle of a shattered nature. My experiences in these places give me the inspiration for my creative activities. Travelling back and forth between my daily life and an old-growth forest will possibly continue for some time for this very reason.

DATA

Date	November, 2000	Aquatic Plants	*Eleocharis acicularis*
Aquarium	W47 x D18 x H24 (in)		*Cryptocoryne balansae*
Lighting	NA Lamp 20W x 12 units, turned on for 10 hours		*Bolbitis heudelotii*
Filter	Super Jet Filter ES-2400, Bio Rio		*Fontinalis antipyretica*
Substrate	Aqua Soil Amazonia, Power Sand L, Bacter 100,	Animals	*Rasbora kalochroma*
	Clear Super, Penac W for Aquarium, Penac P		*Rasbora vaterifloris* var.
CO₂	Pollen Glass Beetle 50, 4 bubbles per second via CO₂		*Rasbora borapetensis*
	Beetle Counter		*Otocinclus* sp.
Aeration	14 hours after the light is turned off using Pollen Glass		*Caridina japonica*
	Beetle 50 for AIR with NA Control Timer		
Additives	Brighty K; Green Brighty STEP 2		
Water Change	1/3 twice a week		
Water Quality	Temperature 79°F; pH 6.8; TH 20mg/l		

DATA

Date	November, 2000
Aquarium	W47 x D18 x H24 (in)
Lighting	NA Lamp 20W x 12 units, turned on for 10 hours
Filte	Super Jet Filter ES-1200, Bio Rio
Substrate	Aqua Soil Amazonia, Sarawak Sand, Power Sand L, Bacter 100, Clear Super, Penac W for Aquarium, Penac P
CO₂	Pollen Glass Beetle 50, 4 bubbles per second via CO₂ Beetle Counter
Aeration	14 hours after the light is turned off using Lily Pipe P-6
Additives	Brighty K; ECA
Water Change	1/4 once a week
Water Quality	Temperature 77°F; pH 6.8; TH 50mg/l
Aqua Plants	*Microsorum* **sp.**
	Eleocharis vivipara
	Cryptocoryne balansae
	Echinodorus angstifolia
	Ludwigia arcuata
	Cyperus helferi
	Blyxa japonica
	Anubias barteri **var.** *barteri*

Vesicularia montagnei
Eleocharis acicularis

Animals *Inpaichthys kerri*
Hemigrammus bleheri
Hyphessobrycon erythrostigma
Nematobrycon palmeri
Pterophyllum scalare
Moenkhausia pittieri
Hyphessobrycon roseus
Hyphessobrycon haraldschultzi
Thoracocharax stellatus
Microgeophagus ramirezi **var.**
Nannobrycon eques
Crossocheilus siamensis

Otocinclus **sp.**
Caridina japonica

DATA

Date	/November, 2000	Water Quality	/Temperature 77°F; pH 6.8; TH 20mg/l
Aquarium	/W71 x D24 x H24 (in)	Aquatic Plants	/*Rotala rotundifolia* (green)
Lighting	/NA Lamp 20W x 24 units, turned on for 10 hours		*Microsorum* sp.
Filter	/External Filter, Bio Rio, NA Carbon 230		*Hygrophila polysperma*
Substrate	/Bright Sand, Power Sand L, Bacter 100, Clear Super,		*Rotala rotundifolia*
	Penac W for Aquarium, Penac P		*Ludwigia* sp.
CO₂	/Pollen Glass Beetle 50 x 2 units, 3 bubbles per		*Rotala wallichii*
	second via CO₂ Beetle Counter x 2 units		*Hygrophila corymbosa*
Aeration	/14 hours after the light is turned off using Lily Pipe P-6	Animals	/*Trigonostigma heteromorpha*
Additives	/Brighty K; Green Brighty STEP 1		*Otocinclus* sp.
Water Change	/1/4 once a week		*Caridina japonica*

The Battle for Survival of Aquatic Plants

An ecosystem in nature exists as a complex relationship between the environment and the living things in it. There exists not only a dog-eat-dog relationship but also battles for survival and changing sceneries. Although this may sound unrelated to an aquarium that is controlled by humans, this is a phenomenon that actually takes place in Nature Aquarium.

This can be explained plainly by the example of several types of stem plants planted densely together in an aquarium. The back-

ground of Nature Aquarium is often planted with stem plants. The growth speeds vary depending on their types, and the difference shows up clearly in their height in a few weeks. If left unattended, slow growing plants become shaded, and they eventually lose the competition and deteriorate. Therefore, it becomes necessary to trim the fast growing plants somewhat early to allow the light to reach all plants evenly. Eventually all plants will develop terminal buds evenly through repeated trimming, and they will form beautiful bushes. Behind their beautiful appearances exists a desperate battle for survival of aquatic plants trying to occupy as much space as possible.

I sometimes use this nature of aquatic plants in an opposite way. I use a lot of stem plants for their showiness and ability to keep water clean when I set up an aquarium. I tuck in *Cryptocoryne* and *Microsorum* among them at that time. In nature, heliophytic aquatic plants that grow fast and require strong light flourish at the beginning. As the light that reaches the bottom surface is blocked gradually, sciophytic plants that grow well under dim light start to increase their presence. Stem plants in the aquarium gradually decline as time passes. By that time, the *Cryptocoryne* and *Microsorum* that were planted among them pick up their pace in an eye-opening speed. A layout created this way ends up looking very different from the design intended by the creator at the beginning. However, a layout that is created naturally over time appears a lot more natural than one that is maintained intentionally by the creator.

DATA

Date	March, 2001
Aquarium	W24 x D12 x H14 (in)
Lighting	NA Lamp 20W x 4 units, turned on for 10 hours
Filter	Super Jet Filter ES-600, Bio Cube 20, Anthracite
Substrate	Aqua Soil Amazonia, Nile Sand, Power Sand S, Bacter 100,
	Clear Super, Penac W for Aquarium, Penac P
CO_2	Pollen Glass, 1 bubble per second via CO_2 Bubble Counter
Aeration	14 hours after the light is turned off using Lily Pipe P-2
Additives	Brighty K
Water Change	1/4 once a week
Water Quality	Temperature 77°F; pH 6.8; TH 20mg/l

Aquatic Plants	*Cryptocoryne retrospiralis*
	Eleocharis acicularis
	Vesicularia montagnei
Animals	*Rasbora agilis*
	Otocinclus **sp.**
	Caridina japonica

DATA

Date	March, 2001
Aquarium	W47 x D18 x H18 (in)
Lighting	NA lamp 40W x 4 units, turned on for 10 hours
Filter	Super Jet Filter ES-1200, Bio Rio
Substrate	Aqua Soil Amazonia, Power Sand Special M, Bacter 100, Clear Super, Penac W for Aquarium, Penac P
CO_2	Pollen Glass Beetle 40, 2 bubbles per second via CO_2 Beetle Counter
Aeration	14 hours after the light is turned off using Pollen Glass Beetle 40 with NA Control Timer
Additives	Brighty K; ECA
Water Change	1/4 once a week
Water Quality	Temperature 77°F; pH 6.8; TH 20mg/l
Aquatic Plants	*Cryptocoryne retrospiralis*
	Cryptocoryne parva
	Cryptocoryne wendtii (green)

Cryptocoryne wendtii (brown)
Eleocharis vivipara
Vesicularia montagnei
Marsilea angustifolia
Cyperus helferi

Animals *Trigonostigma espei*
Rasbora sarawakensis
Rasboroides vaterifloris
Crossocheilus siamensis
Otocinclus sp.
Caridina japonica

DATA

Date	June, 2001
Aquarium	W35 x D18 x H18 (in)
Lighting	NA Lamp 32W x 6 units, turned on for 10 hours
Filter	Super Jet Filter ES-600, Bio Rio, NA Carbon
Substrate	Aqua Soil Amazonia, Power Sand Special M, Penac W for Aquarium, Penac P
CO₂	Pollen Glass Beetle 40, 3 bubbles per second via CO₂ Beetle Counter
Aeration	14 hours after the light is turned off using Lily Pipe P-6
Additives	Brighty K; ECA
Water Change	1/3 once a week
Water Quality	Temperature 77°F; pH 6.8; TH 20mg/l
Aquatic Plants	*Eleocharis acicularis*
	Potamogeton dentatus
	Ludwigia ovaris
	Dysophylla yatabeana
	Acorus gramineus
	Sparganium sp.
	Isoetes japonica
	Sium suave
	Fontinalis antipyretica
Animals	*Oryzias latipes*
	Acheilognathus cyanostigma
	Hemigrammocypris rasborella
	Caridina japonica

DATA

Date / May, 2001

Aquarium / W71 x D24 x H24 (in)

Lighting / NA Lamp 20W x 24 units, turned on for 10 hours

Filter / Super Jet Filter ES-2400, Bio Rio, NA Carbon

Substrate / Aqua Soil Amazonia, Bright Sand, Power Sand L, Bacter 100, Clear Super, Penac W for Aquarium, Penac P

CO₂ / Pollen Glass Beetle 50 x 2 units, 3 bubbles per second via CO₂ Beetle Counter x 2 units

Aeration / 14 hours after the light is turned off using Pollen Glass Beetle 50 for AIR x 2 units

Additives / Brighty K; Green Brighty STEP 2; ECA

Water Change / 1/2 once a week

Water Quality / Temperature 77°F; pH 7.0; TH 20mg/l

Aquatic Plants / Isoetes japonica

Ottelia alismoides

Blyxa japonica

Eleocharis acicularis

Fontinalis antipyretica

Sparganium sp.

Potamogeton dentatus

Animals / Zacco platypus

Otocinclus sp.

Caridina japonica

The Joy of Using Native Japanese Aquatic Plants

The habitats of native Japanese aquatic plants range from a lotic zone, such as rivers, irrigation ditches, and spring fed ponds, to a lentic zone, such as ponds and bogs, and to fallow rice fields. The types of aquatic plants also vary depending on the habitats. *Sparganium* and *Ranunculus nipponicus*, which love pristine, cool water, often dominate spring-fed ponds. Larger varieties of aquatic plants, such as *Potamogeton crispus*, *P. oxyphyllus*, and *Vallisneria asiatica*, grow in nutrient-rich downstream basins. I suppose that many of you readers have seen these aquatic plants flowing in nearby

irrigation ditches. With floating-leaf plants joining the lineup in ponds and bogs, a large amount of aquatic plants grow in clusters in shallow areas where light penetrates well.

However, in recent years, the opportunity to see these aquatic plants has decreased drastically due to the large scale destruction of nature through development, aerial spraying of a large amount of agricultural chemicals, and the pollution of rivers through sewage discharge. When I was a child, beautiful aquatic plants, such as *Ottelia japonica*, *Potamogeton malaianus*, *Aldrovanda vesiculosa*, and *Utricularia*, which are now on the verge of extinction,

grew in various places. Various aquatic insects and beautiful dragonflies also lived in these places in addition to *Zacco platypus*, *Tribolodon hakonensis*, and *Acheilognathus melanogaster* Bleeker.

When you start producing aquatic plant layouts through your own sense of nature, your eyes may be drawn to scenery that did not catch your attention before. You may find unpretentious nature to be quite beautiful. Or, you may get disappointed that nature around you is quickly disappearing. You are likely to rediscover the importance of nature around you even if you don't become passionate enough to demand loudly for nature conservation. If you had an

experience of playing in a pond or river, being absorbed with chasing small fish, it may be fun to reminisce about the past or feel nostalgic over a layout planted with native Japanese aquatic plants. Having the image of the underwater scene that you saw in your childhood reemerge as a real thing is a joy made possible only by a layout with native Japanese plants. My desire to go back to the nature that I knew in my childhood is more or less reflected in the layouts that I produce. That is what makes my work uniquely mine.

DATA
Date / October, 2000
Aquarium / W24 x D12 x H14 (in)
Lighting / NA Lamp 20W x 4 units, turned on for 10 hours
Filte / Super Jet Filter ES-600, Bio Cube, Anthracite
Substrate / Aqua Soil Amazonia, Sarawak Sand, Power Sand S,
Bacter 100, Clear Super, Penac W for Aquarium,

Aeration / 14 hours after the light is turned off using Pollen
Glass for AIR with NA Control Timer
Additives / Brighty K
Water Change / 1/2 once a week
Water Quality / Temperature 77°F; pH 6.6; TH 50mg/l
Aquatic Plants / *Eleocharis acicularis*

DATA
Date / November, 2000
Aquarium / W47 x D18 x H18 (in)
Lighting / NA Lamp 20W x 12 units, turned on for
10 hours
Filter / Super Jet Filter ES-1200, Bio Rio, NA Carbon
Substrate / Aqua Soil Amazonia, Power Sand Special M,
Penac W for Aquarium, Penac P
CO₂ / Pollen Glass Beetle 50, 3 bubbles per second via CO₂
Beetle Counter
Aeration / 14 hours after the light is turned off using Lily Pipe P-6
Additives / Brighty K; ECA
Water Change / 1/3 once a week
Water Quality / Temperature 75°F; pH 6.8; TH 20mg/l
Aquatic Plants / *Eleocharis acicularis*
Hydrocotyle maritima
Bryxa japonica

Sium suave
Isoetes japonica
Ottelia alismoides
Acorus gramineus
Sparganium sp.
Potamogeton malaianus
Animals / *Zacco platypus*
Hemigrammocypris rasborella
Squalidus gracilis gracilis
Caridina japonica

DATA

Date ╱May, 2001

Aquarium╱W71 x D24 x H24 (in)

Lighting ╱NA Lamp 20W x 24 units, turned on for 10 hours

Filter ╱Super Jet Filter ES-2400, Bio Rio L

Substrate╱Aqua Soil Amazonia, Power Sand L, Bacter 100,
Clear Super, Penac W for Aquarium, Penac P

CO₂ ╱Pollen Glass Beetle 50 x 2 units, 2 bubbles per
second via CO₂ Beetle Counter x 2 units

Aeration ╱14 hours after the light is turned off using Lily Pipe P-6

Additives╱Brighty K; ECA

Water Change╱1/3 once a week

Water Quality ╱Temperature 79°F; pH 6.8; TH 50mg/l

Aquatic Plants╱*Echinodorus horemanii*

Echinodorus cordifolius

Echinodorus uruguaiensis

Echinodorus angustifolia

Echinodorus latifolius

Echinodorus tenellus

Animals ╱*Pterophyllum altum*

Nematobrycon palmeri

Hemigrammus bleheri

Hyphessobrycon herbertaxelrodi

Thoracocharax stellatus

Caridina japonica

Otocinclus sp.

DATA

Date	January, 2002
Aquarium	W94.5 x D24 x H24 (in)
Lighting	NA Lamp 40W x 10 units, turned on for 10 hours
Filter	Super Jet Filter ES-2400 x 2 units, Bio Rio, NA Carbon, Tourmaline F
Substrate	Aqua Soil Amazonia, Power Sand Special L, Bacter 100, Clear Super, Penac W for Aquarium, Penac P, Tourmaline BC
CO_2	Pollen Glass Beetle 50 x 2 units, 4 bubbles per second via CO_2 Beetle Counter x 2 units
Aeration	14 hours after the light is turned off using Pollen Glass Beetle 50 for AIR x 2 units
Additives	Brighty K; Green Brighty STEP 2
Water Change	1/2 once a week
Water Quality	Temperature 77°F; pH 6.8; TH 50mg/l
Aquatic Plants	*Glossostigma elatinoides*
	Eleocharis acicularis
	Echinodorus tenellus
Animals	*Trigonostigma heteromorpha*
	Caridina japonica
	Otocinclus sp.

DATA

Date	November, 2001
Aquarium	W71 x D24 x H24 (in)
Lighting	NA Lamp 20W x 24 units, turned on for 10 hours
Filter	Super Jet Filter ES-2400, Bio Rio L, Tourmaline F
Substrate	Aqua Soil Amazonia, Power Sand Special L, Bacter 100, Clear Super, Penac W for Aquarium, Penac P, Tourmaline BC
CO₂	Pollen Glass Beetle 50, 5 bubbles per second via CO₂ Beetle Counter
Aeration	14 hours after the light is turned off using Pollen Glass Beetle 50 for AIR
Additives	Brighty K; Green Brighty STEP 2
Water Change	1/2 once a week
Water Quality	Temperature 77°F; pH 6.8; TH 10mg/l
Aquatic Plants	*Eleocharis acicularis*
Animals	*Paracheirodon simulans*
	Crossocheilus siamensis
	Caridina japonica
	Otocinclus sp.

DATA
Date   July, 2001
Aquarium   W47 x D18 x H18 (in)
Lighting   NA Lamp 20W x 12 units, turned on for 10 hours
Filter   Super Jet Filter ES-1200, Bio Rio

The Challenge to Find a New Rock

I have used various rocks in Nature Aquarium. While these include popular, standard type rocks, such as Hakkai Stone, Manten Stone, and Ryuo Stone, there are some rocks, such as Fuji Stone used in this aquascape, that are becoming hard to obtain. Since rocks are natural materials, they will be gone if they are no longer produced in the area of production. Ohko Stone in the aquascape on the left page is another one of these rocks that we can no longer obtain. Since I cannot tell how long certain rocks are going to be available, I am always looking out for new types of rocks.

There is a basic rock arrangement method for an Iwagumi layout called Sanzon Iwagumi. Even when the same rock arrangement method is used, if the color and texture of rocks are different, the impressions of the overall aquascapes will be different. For this reason it is important to keep looking for new rocks in order to further enhance the variations of Iwagumi layouts.

Although I have used in some layouts types of rocks that are partially

DATA

Date	December, 2001
Aquarium	W47 x D18 x H18 (in)
Lighting	NA Lamp 20W x 12 units, turned on for 10 hours
Filter	Super Jet Filter ES-1200, Bio Rio M, Tourmaline F
Substrate	Aqua Soil Amazonia, Power Sand Special M, Bacter 100, Clear Super, Penac W for Aquarium, Penac P, Tourmaline BC
CO₂	Pollen Glass Beetle 40, 3 bubbles per second via CO₂ Beetle Counter
Aeration	14 hours after the light is turned off using Lily Pipe P-6
Additives	Brighty K; Green Brighty STEP 2
Water Change	1/2 once a week
Water Quality	Temperature 79°F; pH 6.6; TH 20mg/l
Aquatic Plants	*Eleocharis acicularis*
	Glossostigma elatinoides
	Echinodorus tenellus
	Fontinalis antipyretica
Animals	*Trigonostigma heteromorpha*
	Otocinclus sp.
	Caridina japonica

cut or modified, such as Guilin Stone and Keikan Stone, as a general rule I use naturally occurring rocks in Nature Aquarium. Therefore, a new rock must be tested for its ability to affect the water quality before using it for the first time. Since rocks have various origins, their material compositions and abilities to influence the water quality are different depending on the types of rocks. The effect of a rock on the total hardness of water tends to become a problem, especially if aquatic plants are grown with it. The simplest way to check this is to immerse the rock in water and inject CO₂ in the water. Calcium and magnesium that increase the total hardness of water react with water acidified by CO₂ and leach out quickly. Whether the rock will increase the total hardness or not can be found by putting the rock in water and comparing the water hardness before and after adding CO₂ into the water. Because petrified wood that was often used in early Iwagumi layouts was found to increase the total hardness, I developed Softenizer that uses an ion exchange resin as the countermeasure.

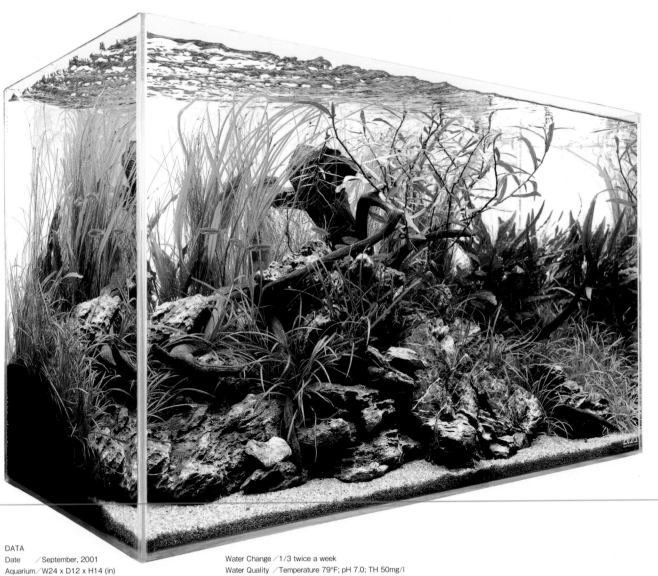

DATA

Date /September, 2001
Aquarium /W24 x D12 x H14 (in)
Lighting /NA Lamp 20W x 4 units, turned on for 10 hours
Filter /Super Jet Filter ES-600, Bio Cube 20, Anthracite
Substrate /Aqua Soil Amazonia, Sarawak Sand, Power Sand S,
　　　　　Bacter 100, Clear Super, Penac W for Aquarium,
　　　　　Penac P
CO₂ /Pollen Glass, 2 bubbles per second via CO₂ Bubble
　　　　　Counter
Aeration /14 hours after the light is turned off using Pollen
　　　　　Glass for AIR with NA Control Timer
Additives /Brighty K; ECA

Water Change /1/3 twice a week
Water Quality /Temperature 79°F; pH 7.0; TH 50mg/l
Aquatic Plants /*Echinodorus tenellus*
　　　　　　　Eleocharis vivipara
　　　　　　　Cryptocoryne albida
　　　　　　　Cryptocoryne petchii
　　　　　　　Isoetes japonica
　　　　　　　Polygonum sp.
Animals /*Cyprinidae* sp.
　　　　　　　Otocinclus sp.
　　　　　　　Caridina japonica

DATA

Date	November, 2001
Aquarium	W47 x D18 x H18 (in)
Lighting	NA Lamp 40W x 4 units, turned on for 10 hours
Filter	Super Jet Filter ES-1200, Bio Rio
Substrate	Aqua Soil Amazonia, Power Sand M, Bacter 100, Clear Super, Penac W for Aquarium, Penac P
CO₂	Pollen Glass Beetle 40, 4 bubbles per second via CO_2 Beetle Counter
Aeration	14 hours after the light is turned off using Pollen Glass Beetle 40 for AIR
Additives	Brighty K
Water Change	1/2 once a week
Water Quality	Temperature 77°F; pH 6.8; TH 20mg/l
Aquatic Plants	*Lilaeopsis novae-zelandiae*
	Cryptocoryne walkeri var. *walkeri*

Cryptocoryne lucens
Cryptocoryne undulata
Cryptocoryne wendtii (brown)
Cryptocoryne wendtii (green)
Sagittaria subulata
Eleocharis vivipara
Hygrophila stricta
Polygonum sp. "pink"
Microsorum sp.

Animals/*Rasbora trilineata*
Trigonostigma heteromorpha
Rasbora borapetensis
Crossocheilus siamensis
Otocinclus sp.
Caridina japonica

DATA

Date	/ September, 2001	Additives / Brighty K; Green Brighty STEP 2; ECA	*Arnoldichthys spilopterus*
Aquarium	/ W71 x D24 x H24 (in)	Water Change / 1/2 once a week	*Otocinclus* **sp.**
Lighting	/ NA Lamp 20W x 24 units, turned on for 10 hours	Water Quality / Temperature 77°F; pH 7.0; TH 20mg/l	*Caridina japonica*
Filter	/ Super Jet Filter ES-2400, Bio Rio, NA Carbon, Tourmaline F	Aquatic Plants / *Anubias barteri* **var.** *nana*	
Substrate	/ Aqua Soil Amazonia, Bright Sand, Power Sand L,	*Anubias barteri* **var.** *barteri*	
	Bacter 100, Clear Super, Penac W for Aquarium, Penac P,	*Bolbitis heudelotii*	
	Tourmaline BC	*Vallisneria spiralis*	
CO₂	/ Pollen Glass Beetle 50 x 2 units, 3 bubbles per second via	*Fontinalis antipyretica*	
	CO₂ Beetle Counter x 2 units	*Cyperus helferi*	
Aeration	/ 14 hours after the light is turned off using Pollen Glass	Animals / *Phenacogrammus interruptus*	
	Beetle 50 for AIR x 2 units	*Bathyaethiops caudomaculatus*	

The Importance of Knowing an Environment

There are many things that I came to understand through finding out about the actual environment of a particular location. The stripes of angelfish, a tropical fish representative of the Amazon, mimic and obscure the fish into the surroundings in an area with a lot of driftwood. Both *Anubias* and *Bolbitis* are aquatic plants representative of West Africa, but no one had seen their natural habitats in the past. When I visited their natural habitats in West Africa, they were growing attached to rocks and driftwood securely

in the same way that I used to grow them in my layouts. This convinced me that my methods were correct. When one lives in a big city, one may get confused and forget that it is not bright outside from morning till night. Therefore, the light over an aquarium may end up being left on all day long. Sciophytic aquatic plants may not be able to tolerate such a condition and melt away. There is a popular type of sciophytic plant called *Cryptocoryne* that is found in Southeast Asia. I wondered why this plant was sciophytic for many years. When I saw its natural habitat, I realized right away.

Cryptocoryne was growing in the bottom of a river in dense woods, under conditions in which light penetrated only for a short time when the sun culminated in the sky. It photosynthesized for such a short time and still grew densely all over the river bottom. After I saw the scene, I came to believe that *Cryptocoryne* did not need much light. Similarly the habitats of *Anubias* and *Bolbitis* that I saw in West Africa were streams in jungles where light penetrated for just a few hours in a day. It is important to find out about the environment of plants by looking at actual locations.

DATA

Date	/ February, 2002	*Cryptocoryne petchii*
Aquarium	/ W35 x D18 x H18 (in)	*Rotala rotundifolia* (green)
Lighting	/ NA Lamp 32W x 6 units, turned on for 10 hours	*Rotala rotundifolia*
Filter	/ Super Jet Filter ES-600, Bio Cube 20, Anthracite	*Rotala wallichii*
Substrate	/ Aqua Soil Amazonia, Power Sand Special M, Bacter 100,	*Rotala macrandra* sp.
	Clear Super, Penac W for Aquarium, Penac P	*Hygrophila polysperma*
CO₂	/ Pollen Glass Beetle 30, 3 bubbles per second via CO₂	*Ludwigia* sp.
	Beetle Counter	*Eleocharis vivipara*
Aeration	/ 14 hours after the light is turned off using Lily Pipe P-4	*Fontinalis antipyretica*
Additives	/ Brighty K; Green Brighty STEP 1; ECA	*Microsorum* sp.
Water Change	/ 1/3 once a week	Animals / *Hyphessobrycon heterorhabdus*
Water Quality	/ Temperature 77°F; pH 6.6; TH 50mg/l	*Inpaichthys kerri*
Aquatic Plants	/ *Lilaeopsis novae-zelandiae*	*Hyphessobrycon sweglesi*
	Eleocharis acicularis	*Thoracocharax stellatus*
	Anubias barteri var. *nana* (narrow)	*Otocinclus* sp.
	Cryptocoryne lucens	*Caridina japonica*

DATA

Date	December, 2001
Aquarium	W24 x D12 x H14 (in)
Lighting	NA Lamp 20W x 4 units, turned on for 10 hours
Filter	Super Jet Filter ES-600, Bio Cube 20, Anthracite, Tourmaline F
Substrate	Aqua Soil Amazonia, Power Sand Special S, Bacter 100, Clear Super, Penac W for Aquarium, Penac P, Tourmaline BC
CO_2	Pollen Glass, 3 bubbles per second via CO_2 Bubble Counter
Aeration	14 hours after the light is turned off using Pollen Glass for AIR
Additives	Brighty K; ECA; Green Gain
Water Change	1/2 once a week
Water Quality	Temperature 77°F; pH 6.8; TH 20mg/l
Aquatic Plants	*Lilaeopsis novae-zelandiae*
	Eleocharis acicularis
	Rotala rotundifolia (green)
	Nesaea pedicellata
	Eusteralis stellata
	Eusteralis sp.
	Hydrocotyle leucocephala
	Rotala rotundifolia
	Rotala macrandra sp.
	Eleocharis vivipara
	Fontinalis antipyretica
	Microsorum sp.
Animals	*Pseudomugil furcatus*
	Hyphessobrycon sweglesi
	Otocinclus sp.
	Caridina japonica

DATA

Date	December, 2001
Aquarium	W24 x D12 x H14 (cm)
Lighting	NA Lamp 20W x 4 units, turned on for 10 hours
Filter	Super Jet Filter ES-600, Bio Cube 20, Anthracite, Tourmaline F
Substrate	Aqua Soil Amazonia, Power Sand S, Bacter 100, Clear Super, Penac W for Aquarium, Penac P, Tourmaline BC
CO_2	Pollen Glass, 2 bubbles per second via CO_2 Bubble Counter
Aeration	14 hours after the light is turned off using Pollen Glass for AIR with NA Control Timer
Additives	Brighty K; Green Brighty STEP 1
Water Change	1/3 once a week
Water Quality	Temperature 79°F; pH 6.8; TH 50mg/l
Aquatic Plants	*Eleocharis acicularis*
Animals	*Inpaichthys kerri*
	Otocinclus sp.
	Crossocheilus siamensis
	Caridina japonica

DATA

Date	September, 2001	Water Change	1/3 once a week		*Rotala rotundifolia* **(green)**
Aquarium	W71 x D24 x H24 (in)	Water Quality	Temperature 77°F; pH 7.0; TH 20mg/l		*Rotala rotundifolia*
Lighting	NA Lamp 20W x 24 units, turned on for 10 hours	Aquatic Plants	*Anubias barteri* **var.** *nana*	Animals	*Trigonostigma heteromorpha*
Filter	Super Jet Filter ES-2400, Bio Rio, NA Carbon,		*Anubias barteri* **var.** *barteri*		*Hyphessobrycon roseus*
	Tourmaline F		*Fontinalis antipyretica*		*Iguanodectes spilurus*
Substrate	Aqua Soil Amazonia, Bright Sand,		*Microsorum* **sp.**		*Thayeria obliqua*
	Power Sand Special L, Bacter 100, Clear Super,		*Bolbitis heudelotii*		*Hemigrammus pulcher*
	Penac W for Aquarium, Penac P, Tourmaline BC		*Hygrophila polysperma*		*Gasteropelecus levis*
CO₂	Pollen Glass Beetle 50 x 2 units, 5 bubbles per		*Eusteralis stellata*		*Hyphessobrycon heterorhabdus*
	second via CO₂ Beetle Counter x 2 units		*Limnophila aquatica*		*Hemigrammus ulreyi*
Aeration	14 hours after the light is turned off using Pollen		*Ludwigia arcuata*		*Hyphessobrycon haraldschultzi*

The Technique of Cosmetic Sand

The white cosmetic sand was introduced into ADA's substrate system by taking a hint from the scenery of the upper Negro river in the Amazon. The water level of the river drops during the dry season, and the scenery of rocks and sand appears on the river bank. The glistening pure white sand washed by the flow of black water along with the rich green color of the tropical rainforest in the background left a spectacular impression in the back of my mind. The white sand bestows an impression of beautiful paradise to the natural scenery. Its effect is demonstrated well by various layouts.

Many aquarists also started expressing land-based landscapes using cosmetic sand some time ago. However, cosmetic sand was used to recreate roads and rivers like in a diorama rather than in an aquascape. Although we all have the freedom to express ourselves, personally I like to put fish in underwater scenery. The star of Nature Aquarium is fish after all, and I believe that its well-balanced natural beauty comes from an aquascape that is enhanced by the presence of fish.

The bottom of the river that I used to dive in was clearly split into places where aquatic plants grew densely and others where no plants grew. In the fallow area next to the places with flowing aquatic plants, the mixture of sand and gravel reflected the light that danced on the water surface. Although sand does not possess the ability to grow aquatic plants, it accentuates the natural feel by its presence in the underwater landscape. It is also fun to dream of the beach in the Amazon or remember a familiar waterfront by using cosmetic sand in a layout.

DATA

Date	╱February, 2002
Aquarium	╱W35 x D18 x H18 (in)
Lighting	╱NA Lamp 32W x 6 units, turned on for 10 hours
Filter	╱Super Jet Filter ES-600, Bio Rio, Tourmaline F
Substrate	╱Aqua Soil Amazonia, Bright Sand, Power Sand M, Bacter 100, Clear Super, Penac W for Aquarium, Penac P, Tourmaline BC
CO₂	╱Pollen Glass Beetle 40, 3 bubbles per second via CO₂ Beetle Counter
Aeration	╱14 hours after the light is turned off using Lily Pipe P-4
Additives	╱Brighty K; Green Brighty STEP 2
Water Change	╱1/3 twice a week
Water Quality	╱Temperature 77°F; pH 7.0; TH 20mg/l
Aquatic Plants	╱*Rotala rotundifolia* (green)
	Rotala wallichii
	Rotala rotundifolia
	Hygrophila polysperma

Ludwigia repens
Pogostemon sp."Dassen"
Cryptocoryne wendtii (green)
Anubias barteri var. *nana*
Anubias barteri var. *nana* (narrow)
Fontinalis antipyretica
Animals╱*Colisa sota* var.
Hyphessobrycon sweglesi
Nannobrycon eques
Nannostomus marginatus
Hyphessobrycon pyrrhonotus
Moenkhausia pittieri
Hyphessobrycon rosaceus var.
Dicrossus maculatus
Otocinclus sp.
Caridina japonica

DATA

Date	/October, 2002	Aquatic Plants	/*Fontinalis antipyretica*
Aquarium	/W35 x D18 x H18 (in)		*Anubias barteri* var. *nana* (narrow)
Lighting	/NA Lamp 32W x 6 units		*Eleocharis acicularis*
Filter	/Super Jet Filter ES-600		*Crinum calamistratum*
Substrate	/Aqua Soil Amazonia, Bright Sand, Power Sand M,	Animals	/*Rasbora agilis*
	Bacter 100, Clear Super, Penac W for Aquarium,		*Otocinclus* sp.
	Penac P, Tourmaline BC		*Caridina japonica*
CO₂	/Pollen Glass Beetle 40, 2 bubbles per second via CO₂		
	Beetle Counter		
Aeration	/14 hours after the light is turned off using Lily Pipe P-4		
Additives	/Brighty K; Green Brighty STEP 2		
Water Change	/1/3 twice a week		
Water Quality	/Temperature 77°F; pH 7.0; TH 50mg/l		

DATA

Date	April, 2002
Aquarium	W47 x D18 x H24 (in)
Lighting	NA Lamp 20W x 12 units, turned on for 10 hours
Filter	Super Jet Filter ES-2400, Bio Rio L, Tourmaline F
Substrate	Aqua Soil, Bright Sand, Power Sand L, Bacter 100, Clear Super, Penac W for Aquarium, Penac P, Tourmaline BC
CO_2	Pollen Glass Beetle 50, 3 bubbles per second via CO_2 Beetle Counter
Aeration	14 hours after the light is turned off using Pollen Glass Beetle 50 for AIR

Additives	Brighty K; Green Brighty STEP 2
Water Change	1/3 once a week
Water Quality	Temperature 77°F; pH 7.0; TH 20mg/l
Aquatic Plants	*Eleocharis acicularis*
	Echinodorus tenellus
	Glossostigma elatinoides
Animals	*Hemigrammus ulreyi*
	Otocinclus sp.
	Caridina japonica

DATA

Date	July, 2001	Water Change	1/4 twice a week
Aquarium	W35 x D18 x H18 (in)	Water Quality	Temperature 77°F; pH 7.0; TH 50mg/l
Lighting	NA Lamp 32W x 6 units	Aquatic Plants	*Cryptocoryne retrospiralis*
Filter	Super Jet Filter ES-600, Bio Rio, Tourmaline F		*Microsorum* sp.
Substrate	Aqua Soil Amazonia, Bright Sand, Power Sand M,		*Eleocharis acicularis*
	Bacter 100, Clear Super, Penac W for Aquarium,		*Vesicularia montagnei*
	Penac P, Tourmaline BC	Animals	*Trigonostigma heteromorpha*
CO₂	Pollen Glass Beetle 30, 2 bubbles per second via CO₂		*Otocinclus* sp.
	Beetle Counter		*Caridina japonica*
Aeration	14 hours after the light is turned off using Lily Pipe P-4		

DATA

Date	October, 2002	Water Quality	Temperature 79°F; pH 6.8; TH 50mg/l	Animals	*Melanotaenia praecox*
Aquarium	W35 x D18 x H18 (in)	Aquatic Plants	*Rotala rotundifolia* (green)		*Gasteropelecus sternicla*
Lighting	NA Lamp 32W x 6 units, turned on for 10 hours		*Rotala rotundifolia*		*Inpaichthys kerri*
Filter	Super Jet Filter ES-600, Bio Rio, Tourmaline F		*Rotala* sp.		*Hyphessobrycon rosaceus*
Substrate	Aqua Soil Amazonia, Bright Sand, Power Sand M,		*Rotala wallichii*		*Nannobrycon eques*
	Bacter 100, Clear Super, Penac W for Aquarium,		*Rotala nanjean*		*Hyphessobrycon haraldschultzi*
	Penac P, Tourmaline BC		*Eleocharis vivipara*		*Otocinclus* sp.
CO₂	Pollen Glass Beetle 40, 3 bubbles per second via CO₂		*Fontinalis antipyretica*		*Caridina japonica*
	Beetle Counter		*Microsorum* sp.		
Aeration	14 hours after the light is turned off using Lily Pipe P-6		*Polygonum* sp."pink"		
Additives	Brighty K; Green Brighty STEP 2; ECA		*Hydrocotyle leucocephala*		
Water Change	1/3 once a week		*Cryptocoryne albida*		

Aquarium Sizes and the Film Format

I have created thousands of layouts up to now. The sizes of these aquariums varied greatly. I created aquascapes with densely growing aquatic plants and fish in aquariums that are hugely different in scales, from the tiniest 1.2-inch cube aquarium up to a 16-foot-long super-sized aquarium. I called the aquascape in the tiniest aquarium "Shouchu Suikei (an aquascape that fits in a hand)." The aquarium small enough to fit in a hand, which I created with minute details by laying sand, putting in a rock, and planting aquatic plants, had great reactions from home and abroad. However, it was too small an environment to keep fish in and difficult to maintain long term. On the other hand, a super sized aquarium requires a layout that can be maintained for a long time since it cannot be

reworked easily. Therefore, it requires careful planning from the early stage of selecting layout materials and aquatic plants.

Although most aquarium sizes do not vary to that extreme, various sized aquariums are on display in Nature Aquarium Gallery. Just the Cube Gardens alone range from foot-wide mini aquariums up to 6-foot-wide large aquariums. Since the aspect ratio of an aquarium varies depending on the size of the aquarium, the impression of an aquascape varies greatly as well. The selection of an aquarium for an aquascape somewhat resembles the selection of film format for a photograph. The large format films that I use for aquascape photographs and landscape photographs come in a variety of formats, such as 8 x 20 and 5 x 7 inch formats. In the case of landscape photographs, I normally take photographs

with 5 x 7 inch format films, but when I want to express the panoramic view of a sprawling landscape, I use 8 x 20 inch format films. I choose films based on the type of scenery and my intended expression. Similarly, in the case of an aquarium, I choose the method of expression based on the aquarium. For example, I express a sprawling panoramic view in an aquarium with a wide aspect ratio. As an aquarium becomes smaller, even if the aspect ratio stays the same, minor flaws and roughness tend to stand out. On the other hand, as an aquarium becomes larger, an aquascape can be produced with greater attention to detail. This is similar to the fact that finer details can be rendered more clearly as the film format increases in size. My insistence on the attention to detail is at the root of my expression.

DATA

Date	October, 2002
Aquarium	W47 x D18 x H24 (in)
Lighting	NA Lamp 20W x 12 units, turned on for 10 hours
Filter	Super Jet Filter ES-1200, Bio Rio
Substrate	Aqua Soil Amazonia, Power Sand L, Bacter 100, Clear Super, Penac W for Aquarium, Penac P, Tourmaline BC
CO₂	Pollen Glass Beetle 50, 3 bubbles per second via CO₂ Beetle Counter
Aeration	14 hours after the light is turned off using Lily Pipe P-6
Additives	Brighty K; Green Brighty STEP 2
Water Change	1/3 twice a week
Water Quality	Temperature 77°F; pH 6.6; TH 50mg/l
Aquatic Plants	*Fontinalis antipyretica*
	Microsorum sp.
	Glossostigma elatinoides
	Eleocharis acicularis
	Echinodorus tenellus
	Vallisneria kauresen
Animals	*Hyphessobrycon megalopterus*
	Crossocheilus siamensis
	Otocinclus sp.
	Caridina japonica

DATA

Date / December, 2002

Aquarium / W35 x D18 x H18 (in)

Lighting / NA Lamp 32W x 6 units, turned on for 10 hours

Filter / Super Jet Filter ES-600, Bio Rio

Substrate / Aqua Soil Amazonia, Bright Sand, Power Sand M,
Bacter 100, Clear Super, Penac W for Aquarium,
Penac P, Tourmaline BC

CO₂ / Pollen Glass Beetle 40, 4 bubbles per second via CO₂
Beetle Counter

Aeration / 14 hours after the light is turned off using Lily Pipe P-4

Additives / Brighty K; Green Brighty STEP 2; ECA

Water Change / 1/3 once a week

Water Quality / Temperature 77°F; pH 6.8; TH 20mg/l

Aquatic Plants / *Fontinalis antipyretica*
Microsorum sp.
Rotala rotundifolia (green)
Eleocharis vivipara

Anmals / *Hyphessobrycon haraldschultzi*
Caridina japonica
Otocinclus sp.

DATA

Date	/December, 2002
Aquarium	/W35 x D18 x H18 (in)
Lighting	/NA Lamp 32W x 6 units, turned on for 10 hours
Filter	/Super Jet Filter ES-600, Bio Cube, Anthracite,
Substrate	/Aqua Soil Amazonia, Bright Sand, Power Sand M, Bacter 100, Clear Super, Penac W for Aquarium, Penac P, Tourmaline BC
CO₂	/Pollen Glass Beetle 40, 4 bubbles per second via CO₂ Beetle Counter
Aeration	/14 hours after the light is turned off using Lily Pipe P-4
Additives	/Brighty K; Green Brighty STEP 2; ECA
Water Change	/1/3 once a week
Water Quality	/Temperature 77°F; pH 6.8; TH 20mg/l

Aquatic Plants /*Riccia fluitans*
Fontinalis antipyretica
Hydrocotyle maritima
Rotala macrandra sp.
Rotala rotundifolia
Rotala nanjean
Ludwigia arcuata
Rotala rotundifolia (green)
Rotala sp.
Microsorum sp.

Animals /*Paracheirodon simulans*
Hemigrammus bleheri
Hemigrammus pulcher
Caridina japonica
Otocinclus sp.

DATA

Date	October, 2002
Aquarium	W47 x D18 x H24 (in)
Lighting	NA Lamp 20W x 12 units, turned on for 10 hours
Filter	Super Jet Filter ES-2400, Bio Rio
Substrate	Aqua Soil Amazonia, Power Sand L, Bacter 100, Clear Super, Penac W for Aquarium, Penac P, Tourmaline BC
CO₂	Pollen Glass Beetle 50, 4 bubbles per second via CO₂ Beetle Counter
Aeration	14 hours after the light is turned off using Lily Pipe P-6
Additives	Brighty K; Green Brighty STEP 1

Water Change	1/3 once a week
Water Quality	Temperature 77°F; pH 6.8; TH 20mg/l
Aquatic Plants	*Eleocharis acicularis*
	Echinodoarus tenellus
	Glossostigma elatinoides
Animals	*Trigonostigma heteromorpha*
	Otocinclus sp.
	Caridina japonica

The New Expression of Iwagumi Layout

My dream of using a school of Cardinal Tetras in a densely planted 120 cm aquarium was realized quite accidentally. It was about 30 years ago, around the time *Echinodorus tenellus* was just brought into Japan. The *E. tenellus* that I got hold of at that time was spindly, like alfalfa sprouts, and hardly looked like what you see today. Since I thought that the plant would look forlorn in a 47-inch-aquarium by itself, I picked up the river rocks that I had and arranged them casually in the aquarium. I got carried away and finished it into a completed layout in the end. Although I often used rocks in a layout in the past, this was the start of a full-fledged Iwagumi layout.

The combination of a single type of plant and a single type of fish is the most basic style of an Iwagumi layout. I call this "Tanshoku Tanei (single plant single fish)." I continue to produce this style Iwagumi layout, although the type of plant now extends to *Glossostigma*, hair grass, *Riccia*, and *Hemianthus callitricoides*. The use of a single type of plant expresses the appeal of Iwagumi itself the most directly.

Several types of aquatic plants are sometimes grown together in an Iwagumi layout. This helps to modify the strength of rocks and increases the natural feel of the layout. Multiple types of short growing aquatic plants, the same types of plants that are used in a layout with a single type of plant, are used as the primary plants in this case, too. Somewhat taller hair grass or *E. tenellus* is used behind or around rocks and shorter *Glossostigma* or *H. callitricoides* is used in front of them. This style utilizes the hierarchical structure of plants seen in nature, which helps to enhance perspective along with soil mounding.

There is another one with cosmetic sand placed around rockwork. Although some people may associate it with Karesansui of Japanese Gardens, it actually originates from the view of white sand and rocks in the banks of the Amazon.

DATA

Date	October, 2002
Aquarium	W35 x D18 x H18 (in)
Lighting	NA Lamp 32W x 6 units, turned on for 10 hours
Filter	Super Jet Filter ES-600, Bio Rio
Substrate	Aqua Soil Amazonia, Power Sand M, Bacter 100, Clear Super, Penac W for Aquarium, Penac P, Tourmaline BC
CO₂	Pollen Glass Beetle 40, 2 bubbles per second via CO₂ Beetle Counter
Aeration	14 hours after the light is turned off using Pollen Glass Beetle 40 for AIR
Additives	Brighty K; Green Brighty STEP 2
Water Change	1/2 once a week
Water Quality	Temperature 77°F; pH 6.8; TH 20mg/l
Aquatic Plants	*Eleocharis acicularis*
	Fontinalis antipyretica
Animals	*Inpaichthys kerri*
	Otocinclus sp.
	Caridina japonica

DATA

Date／December, 2002

Aquarium／W71 x D24 x H24 (in)

Lighting／NAMH-150W (Solar I) x 3 units, turned on for 10 hours

Filter／Super Jet Filter ES-2400, Bio Rio

Substrate／Aqua Soil Amazonia, Power Sand Special L,
Bacter 100, Clear Super, Penac W for Aquarium,
Penac P, Tourmaline BC

CO₂／Pollen Glass Beetle 50, 4 bubbles per second via CO₂
Beetle Counter

Aeration／14 hours after the light is turned off using Lily Pipe P-6

Additives／Brighty K; Green Brighty STEP 2

Water Change／1/3 twice a week

Water Quality／Temperature 77°F; pH 6.8; TH 50mg/l

Aquatic Plants／*Fontinalis antipyretica*
Lilaeopsis novae-zelandiae

Animals／*Iguanodectes spilurus*
Otocinclus sp.
Caridina japonica

Selection of Aquatic Plants and Fish

When I select aquatic plants for a layout, I select them not only by their sizes and growth habits but particularly by focusing on their colors. Some aquatic plants are green and some are red. Plants come in various shades of red. Some are purplish, and some are orangish. Just like paints, they come in many colors. The impression of a layout changes greatly depending on how you use the multitude of colors. After the framework of a composition is established with driftwood and rocks, coloring is done with aquatic plants. Up to this point, the process may feel similar to painting a picture. In the case of fish, not only colors but also their body shapes and movements are important. Slender fish match an Iwagumi layout produced in the image of vast grassland. On the other hand, fish that swim in a fluttering manner go together well with a layout produced with driftwood in the image of dense woods. While an Iwagumi layout with a wide open space may feel refreshing in summer, one may find warmth in a layout with stem plants that resembles dense woods in winter. I see a diorama style layout that strongly resembles a land-based landscape quite often lately. The success of this type of work seems to depend on whether it looks good with fish or not. Not using fish at all may be an option for such a layout. Although I do not particularly care for it, I think that it is fine to have such an expression. Aside from the problem of fish, expanding the aquarium hobby by setting a new genre is a welcome development. I feel that it is great that many people think about and debate on the expression of a layout, which is also an environment of living things, along the way.

Rapidly Changing Environment of the Amazon

Learning from nature is at the origin of Nature Aquarium philosophy. A new creation is not brought to life without actually looking at nature. However, the nature I knew in my childhood no longer exists in nearby places. So, I went to the Amazon wearing my goggles in search of unspoiled nature and explored in detail the underwater world of rivers and marshes. Although the types of fish and aquatic plants were different, there existed a rich, natural, underwater world that has something in common with the memories of the streams and lagoon of my childhood.

I played in water as if I was a child again. I gulped river water, hurt my foot with driftwood, and got scratches on my face and limbs going through weeds. I was stung by mosquitoes and ticks, too. Nature has many faces. It is not only beautiful, but it is also kind, though strict, sometimes. When I put myself in nature, I can feel it all over my body. So I went to the Amazon many times and recharged myself fully with the energy of nature.

The Amazon is getting seriously damaged since the demand for bioethanol intensified seven years ago. The last time I visited the Amazon, a huge amount of ashes were collecting in the watershed areas. Tropical rainforests of the Amazon equivalent to the size of Shikoku Island are said to be disappearing every year due to logging and slash-and-burn agriculture. Where did the ashes from the huge amount of trees go? The ashes were washed into rivers by rains and then spread to various places. The ashes in the water polluted the environment and threatened the lives of many aquatic organisms. The white, sandy beaches of the Negro River were soiled with ashes and looked nothing like what they once did.

Such a change is happening in many places in the Amazon. I have not visited the Amazon since that time because I do not want to photograph the devastation of nature that was once so beautiful.

DATA

Date	/ March, 2002
Aquarium	/ W71 x D47 x H31.5 (in)
Lighting	/ NA Lamp 40W x 4 units, NA Lamp 20W x 14 units turned on for 10 hours
Filter	/ Original External Filter, Bio Rio
Substrate	/ Aqua Soil Amazonia, Sarawak Sand, Power Sand Special L, Bacter 100, Clear Super, Penac W for Aquarium, Penac P, Tourmaline BC
CO₂	/ Pollen Glass Beetle 50 x 2 units, 4 bubbles per second via CO₂ Beetle Counter x 2 units
Additives	/ Brighty K; Green Brighty STEP 2

Water Change	/ 1/3 twice a week
Water Quality	/ Temperature 81°F; pH 6.4; TH 20mg/l
Aquatic Plants	/ *Vallisneria neotropicalis*
	Sagittaria graminea var. *platyphylla*
	Echinodorus argentinensis
Animals	/ *Symphysodon* sp. **Heckel**
	Pterophyllum scalare
	Mesonauta festivus
	Otocinclus sp.
	Crossocheilus siamensis
	Caridina japonica

DATA

Date	July, 2003
Aquarium	W35 x D18 x H24 (in)
Lighting	NAMH-150W (Solar I) x 1.5 units, turned on for 10 hours
Filter	Super Jet Filter ES-1200
Substrate	Aqua Soil Amazonia, Power Sand Special L, Bacter 100, Clear Super, Penac W for Aquarium, Penac P, Tourmaline BC
CO₂	Pollen Glass Large 30, 4 bubbles per second via CO₂ Beetle Counter
Aeration	14 hours after the light is turned off using Lily Pipe P-4

Additives	Brighty K; Green Brighty STEP 2; ECA
Water Change	1/3 once a week
Water Quality	Temperature 77°F; pH 6.8; TH 10mg/l
Aquatic Plants	*Lilaeopsis novae-zelandiae*
	Anubias barteri var. *nana*
	Eusteralis stellata
	Rotala wallichii
	Ludwigia arcuata
	Rotala rotundifolia (green)
	Rotala rotundifolia

	Rotala nanjean
	Rotala macrandra sp.
	Rotala macrandra sp.
Animals	*Hemigrammus pulcher*
	Caridina japonica
	Otocinclus sp.

DATA

Date	/ January, 2003
Aquarium	/ W24 x D12 x H14 (in)
Lighting	/ NA Lamp 20W x 4 units, turned on for 10 hours
Filter	/ Super Jet Filter ES-600, Bio Cube, Anthracite
Substrate	/ Aqua Soil Amazonia, Power Sand Special S, Bacter 100, Clear Super, Penac W for Aquarium, Penac P, Tourmaline BC
CO_2	/ Pollen Glass, 3 bubbles per second via CO_2 Bubble Counter
Aeration	/ 14 hours after the light is turned off using Lily Pipe P-2
Additives	/ Brighty K; Green Brighty STEP 2
Water Change	/ 1/3 once a week
Water Quality	/ Temperature 77°F; pH 7.0; TH 20mg/l
Aquatic Plants	/ *Glossostigma elatinoides*
	Fontinalis antipyretica
	Riccia fluitans
	Microsorum sp.
	Rotala rotundifolia
	Rotala rotundifolia (green)
	Rotala macrandra sp.
	Ludwigia arcuata
	Micranthemum unbrosum
	Anubias barteri var. *nana* (narrow)
Animals	/ *Poecilia reticulata* var.
	Poecilia reticulata var.
	Caridina japonica
	Otocinclus sp.

DATA

Date	/ March, 2002
Aquarium	/ W24 x D12 x H14 (in)
Lighting	/ NA Lamp 20W x 4 units, turned on for 10 hours
Filter	/ Super Jet Filter ES-600, Bio Cube, Anthracite
Substrate	/ Aqua Soil Amazonia, Power Sand S, Bacter 100, Clear Super, Penac W for Aquarium, Penac P, Tourmaline BC
CO_2	/ Pollen Glass, 3 bubbles per second via CO_2 Bubble Counter
Aeration	/ 14 hours after the light is turned off using Pollen Glass for AIR with NA Control Timer
Additives	/ Brighty K; Green Brighty Special LIGHTS; ECA
Water Chang	/ 1/3 twice a week
Water Quality	/ Temperature 79°F; pH 6.6; TH 20mg/l
Aquatic Plants	/ *Glossostigma elatinoides*
	Riccia fluitans
Animals	/ *Pterophyllum scalare*
	Hyphessobrycon elachys
	Caridina japonica
	Otocinclus sp.

DATA

Date   March, 2001

Aquarium   W24 x D12 x H14 (in)

Lighting   NA Lamp 20W x 4 units, turned on for 10 hours

Filter   Super Jet Filter ES-600, Bio Cube, Anthracite

Water Change   1/2 once a week

Water Quality   Temperature 77°F; pH 6.8; TH 20mg/l

Aquatic Plants   *Glossostigma elatinoides*

           Echinodorus tenellus

DATA
Date   July, 2003
Aquarium   W47 x D18 x H18 (in)
Lighting   NA Lamp 20W x 12 units, turned on for 10 hours
Filter   Super Jet Filter ES-1200, Bio Rio
Substrate   Aqua Soil Amazonia, Sarawak Sand,
              Power Sand Special M, Bacter 100, Clear Super,
              Penac W for Aquarium, Penac P   Aquatic Plants   *Glossostigma elatinoides*
CO₂   Pollen Glass Beetle 40, 4 bubbles per second via CO₂   *Echinodorus tenellus*
              Beetle Counter   *Ludwigia arcuata*
Aeration   14 hours after the light is turned off using Lily Pipe P-6   Animals   *Paracheirodon simulans*
Additives   Brighty K; Green Brighty STEP 1   *Caridina japonica*
Water Change 1/3 once a week   *Crossocheilus siamensis*
Water Quality Temperature 75°F; pH 6.8; TH 20mg/l   *Otocinclus* sp.

DATA

Date	/July, 2003	Aquatic Plants	/*Glossostigma elatinoides*
Aquarium	/W35 x D18 x H18 (in)		*Eleocharis acicularis*
Lighting	/NA Lamp 32W x 6 units, turned on for 10 hours	Animals	/*Trigonostigma espei*
Filter	/Super Jet Filter ES-600, Bio Rio		*Caridina japonica*
Substrate	/Aqua Soil Amazonia, Power Sand Special M,		*Otocinclus* sp.
	Bacter 100, Clear Super, Penac W for Aquarium,		
	Penac P, Tourmaline BC		
CO₂	/Pollen Glass Large 30, 3 bubbles per second via CO₂		
	Beetle Counter		
Aeration	/14 hours after the light is turned off using Lily Pipe P-4		
Additives	/Brighty K; Green Brighty STEP 2		
Water Change	/1/3 once a week		
Water Quality	/Temperature 77°F; pH 7.0; TH 10mg/l		

DATA
Date /July, 2003
Aquarium /W47 x D18 x H24 (in)
Lighting /NAMH-150W (Solar I) x 2 units, turned on for 10 hours
Filter /Super Jet Filter ES-1200, Bio Rio M, NA Carbon
Substrate /Aqua Soil Amazonia, Power Sand Special L,
Bacter 100, Clear Super, Penac W for Aquarium,
Penac P, Tourmaline BC
CO₂ /Pollen Glass Beetle 40, 3 bubbles per second via CO₂
Beetle Counter
Aeration /14 hours after the light is turned off using Lily Pipe P-4
Additives /Brighty K; Green Brighty STEP 2; ECA
Water Change /1/3 once a week
Water Quality /Temperature 76°F; pH 7.0; TH 10mg/l

Aquatic Plants/*Lilaeopsis novae-zelandiae*
Rotala rotundifolia (green)
Ludwigia arcuata
Polygonum sp. "pink"
Microsorum sp.
Fontinalis antipyretica
Animals /*Hemigrammus ocellifer*
Otocinclus sp.
Caridina japonica

DATA

Date	January, 2003
Aquarium	W22 x D22 x H22 (in)
Lighting	NAMH-150W, turned on for 10 hours
Filter	Super Jet Filter ES-600, Bio Rio
Substrate	Aqua Soil Amazonia, Bright Sand, Power Sand Special M, Bacter 100, Clear Super, Penac W for Aquarium, Penac P, Tourmaline BC
CO₂	Pollen Glass Beetle 30, 2 bubbles per second via CO₂ Beetle Counter
Aeration	14 hours after the light is turned off using Lily Pipe P-4
Additives	Brighty K; Green Brighty STEP 2
Water Change	1/3 once a week
Water Quality	Temperature 77°F; pH 6.6; TH 20mg/l
Aquatic Plants	*Fontinalis antipyretica*
	Microsorum **sp.**
	Ottelia ulvifolia
Animals	*Melanotaenia maccullochi*
	Caridina japonica
	Otocinclus **sp.**
	Corydoras **sp.**

DATA

Date	January, 2003
Aquarium	W22 x D22 x H22 (in)
Lighting	NAMH-150W (Solar I), turned on for 10 hours
Filter	Super Jet Filter ES-600, Bio Rio
Substrate	Aqua Soil Amazonia, Bright Sand, Power Sand Special M, Bacter 100, Clear Super, Penac W for Aquarium, Penac P, Tourmaline BC
CO₂	Pollen Glass Beetle 30, 3 bubbles per second via CO₂ Beetle Counter
Aeration	14 hours after the light is turned off using Lily Pipe P-4
Additives	Brighty K; Green Brighty STEP 2
Water Change	1/3 once a week
Water Quality	Temperature 77°F; pH 6.8; TH 20mg/l
Aquatic Plants	*Fontinalis antipyretica*
	Microsorum **sp.**
	Bolbitis heudelotii
	Hygrophila polysperma
Animals	*Trigonostigma heteromorpha*
	Crossocheilus siamensis
	Caridina japonica
	Otocinclus **sp.**

DATA

Date /July, 2003
Aquarium /W35 x D18 x H24 (in)
Lighting /NAG-150W Green/NA Twin 36W (Grand Solar I),
           turned on for 10 hours
Filter /Super Jet Filter ES-1200, Bio Rio
Substrate /Aqua Soil Amazonia, Rio Negro Sand,
           Power Sand Special L, Bacter 100, Clear Super,
           Penac W for Aquarium, Penac P, Tourmaline BC
CO₂ /Pollen Glass Large 30, 4 bubbles per second via CO₂
     Beetle Counter

Aeration /14 hours after the light is turned off using Lily Pipe P-4
Additives /Brighty K; Green Brighty STEP 2
Water Change /1/3 once a week
Water Quality /Temperature 75°F; pH 6.8; TH 10mg/l
Aquatic Plants /Wabi-Kusa Stemmed Plants MIX
              Microsorum sp.
              Fontinalis antipyretica
              Cryptocoryne petchii
              Cryptocoryne wendtii (green × tall form)
              Hedera helix var.

Animals /*Hemigrammus armstrongi*
        Crossocheilus siamensis
        Caridina japonica
        Otocinclus sp.

DATA

Date	September, 2005	Aeration	14 hours after the light is turned off using Lily Pipe P-4	*Cryptocoryne petchii*
Aquarium	W35 x D18 x H24 (in)	Additives	Brighty K; Green Brighty STEP 2	*Cryptocoryne pontederifolia*
Lighting	NAG-150W Green/NA Lamp Twin 36W (Grand Solar I), turned on for 10 hours	Water Change	1/3 once a week	*Hedera helix* var.
		Water Quality	Temperature 75°F; pH 6.8; TH 10mg/l	*Philodendron oxycardium*
Filter	Super Jet Filter ES-1200, Bio Rio	Aquatic Plants	Wabi-Kusa Stemmed Plants MIX	Animals / *Paracheirodon innesi*
Substrate	Aqua Soil Amazonia, Rio Negro Sand, Power Sand Special L, Bacter 100, Clear Super, Penac W for Aquarium, Penac P, Tourmaline BC		Wabi-Kusa Echinodorus-Cryptocoryne MIX	*Crossocheilus siamensis*
			Microsorum sp.	*Caridina japonica*
			Bolbitis heudelotii	*Otocinclus* sp.
CO₂	Pollen Glass Large 30, 3 bubbles per second via CO₂ Beetle Counter		*Fontinalis antipyretica*	
			Eleocharis acicularis	

DATA

Date	July, 2003	Additives	Brighty K
Aquarium	W71 x D24 x H24 (in)	Water Change	1/3 once a week
Lighting	NAMH-150W (Solar I) x 3 units, turned on for 10 hours	Water Quality	Temperature 77°F; pH 7.2; TH 50mg/l
Filter	Super Jet Filter ES-2400, Bio Rio	Aquatic Plants	*Fontinalis antipyretica*
Substrate	Aqua Soil Amazonia, Power Sand Special L,	Animals	*Paracheirodon axelrodi*
	Bacter 100, Clear Super, Penac W for Aquarium,		*Caridina japonica*
	Penac P, Tourmaline BC		*Otocinclus* sp.
CO₂	Pollen Glass Beetle 50, 4 bubbles per second via CO₂		
	Beetle Counter		
Aeration	14 hours after the light is turned off using Lily Pipe P-6		

An Iwagumi that Expresses Majestic Scenery

I draw on the scenery of rivers and oceans primarily for creating rock arrangements in an Iwagumi layout. The scenery of a river offers many useful references for certain details of rock arrangement and soil mounding, such as the position and tilt of rocks that are influenced by the flow of water and the way that pebbles and sand accumulate around rocks. The scenery of the ocean offers great references in a much larger scale, such as the formation and balance of rocks and the breadth of scenery. Many wild landscapes are seen on the ocean front with rocks

DATA

Date	╱November, 2003
Aquarium	╱W35 x D18 x H18 (in)
Lighting	╱NA Lamp 32W x 6 units, turned on for 10 hours
Filter	╱Super Jet Filter ES-600, Bio Rio
Substrate	╱Aqua Soil Amazonia, Power Sand M, Bacter 100, Clear Super, Penac W for Aquarium, Penac P, Tourmaline BC
CO₂	╱Pollen Glass Large 30, 3 bubbles per second via CO₂ Beetle Counter
Aeration	╱14 hours after the light is turned off using Lily Pipe P-4
Additives	╱Brighty K; Green Brighty STEP 1

Water Change	╱1/3 once a week
Water Quality	╱Temperature 77°F; pH 7.0; TH 20mg/l
Aquatic Plants	╱*Riccia fluitans*
	Rotala rotundifolia (green)
	Glossostigma elatinoides
Animals	╱*Hyphessobrycon pyrrhonotus*
	Thayeria boehlkei
	Nematobrycon palmeri
	Gasteropelecus sternicla
	Caridina japonica
	Otocinclus sp.

DATA

Date / November, 2003

Aquarium / W24 x D12 x H14 (in)

Lighting / NA Lamp 20W x 4 units, turned on for 10 hours

Filter / Super Jet Filter ES-600, Bio Rio

Substrate / Aqua Soil Amazonia, Power Sand Special S, Bacter 100, Clear Super, Penac W for Aquarium, Penac P, Tourmaline BC

CO₂ / Pollen Glass, 3 bubbles per second via CO₂ Bubble Counter

Aeration / 14 hours after the light is turned off using Lily Pipe P-2

Additives / Brighty K; Green Brighty STEP 2

Water Change / 1/3 once a week

Water Quality / Temperature 79°F; pH 6.8; TH 20mg/l

Aquatic Plants / *Marsilea crenata*

Fontinalis antipyretica

Eleocharis vivipara

Cryptocoryne wendtii (green)

Cryptocoryne petchii

Animals / *Chela dadyburjori*

Caridina japonica

Otocinclus sp.

DATA

		Water Quality	Temperature 75°F; pH 6.8; TH 10mg/l
Date	July, 2003	Aquatic Plants	*Glossostigma elatinoides*
Aquarium	W71 x D24 x H24 (in)		*Riccia fluitans*
Lighting	NAMH-150W (Solar I) x 3 units, turned on for 10 hours		*Blyxa japonica*
Filter	Super Jet Filter ES-2400, Bio Rio		*Echinodorus tenellus*
Substrate	Aqua Soil Amazonia, Power Sand Special L,		*Eleocharis acicularis*
	Bacter 100, Clear Super, Penac W for Aquarium,		*Eleocharis vivipara*
	Penac P, Tourmaline BC	Animals	*Nematobrycon lacortei*
CO₂	Pollen Glass Beetle 50, 7 bubbles per second via CO₂		*Nematobrycon palmeri*
	Beetle Counter		*Otocinclus sp.*
Aeration	14 hours after the light is turned off using Lily Pipe P-6		*Caridina japonica*
Additives	Brighty K, Green Brighty STEP 2, ECA		
Water Change	1/3 once a week		

The Reason for Creating the Gallery

The Nature Aquarium Gallery was built inside of the ADA Head-quarters building. It is open to the public on holidays. The big reason for opening the gallery was the fact that more and more people from both home and abroad wanted to come and see the actual aquascapes in person as Nature Aquarium became popular in the world. The aquascape photographs, which were published in photo books and magazines, were what made Nature Aquarium popular worldwide in the first place. The aquascapes that were published up to that point were photographs of aquariums installed in satellite shops and lobbies of offices. Since the

number of aquariums available for public viewing at one time was limited in this way, we decided to open up a larger space to place as many aquariums as possible for public viewing, and this also served as a showroom for our products as the number of requests increased.

Thus Nature Aquarium Gallery was born in July 2003. Approximately forty aquariums, large and small, are on display at all times. This may be the only place in the world that has this many aquatic plant layouts on display. Since the Gallery opened, many visitors have come not only from within Japan, but also from overseas on holidays.

Another reason for building the Gallery is to prove the effectiveness of the system that was developed to maintain Nature Aquarium and also to exemplify the fact that it is possible to maintain layouts for a long period of time. Nature Aquarium System was developed to grow healthy aquatic plants and fish in an aquarium and to maintain them for a long period of time. If only the photographs of newly created aquascapes were published, it might have led to the misunderstanding that such layouts cannot be maintained for long time. I also wanted the Gallery to be a place not only to display the basic equipment setup and demonstrate water changes, but also to demonstrate

and do research on trimming and fertilization of aquatic plants. In actuality, the aquascapes in the Gallery are maintained for long periods of time and the ADA staff provides explanations for the system functions and the maintenance methods. I feel that the Gallery is also a place where we can directly show what goes on behind the scenes of maintaining the layouts, something that is difficult to understand from the photographs and articles published in magazines alone.

DATA

Date	╱ April, 2002
Aquarium	╱ W47 x D18 x H18 (in)
Lighting	╱ NA Lamp 20W x 12 units, turned on for 10 hours
Filter	╱ Super Jet Filter ES-1200, Bio Rio
Substrate	╱ Aqua Soil Amazonia, Power Sand Special M,
	Bacter 100, Clear Super, Penac W for Aquarium, Penac P
CO_2	╱ Pollen Glass Beetle 40, 5 bubbles per second via CO_2
	Beetle Counter
Aeration	╱ 14 hours after the light is turned off using Lily Pipe P-6
Additives	╱ Brighty K; Green Brighty STEP 2
Water Change	╱ 1/3 once a week

Water Quality	╱ Temperature 77°F; pH 6.6; TH 20mg/l
Aquatic Plants	╱ *Riccia fluitans*
	Glossostigma elatinoides
	Eleocharis acicularis
	Blyxa japonica
	Echinodorus tenellus
Animals	╱ *Bathyaethiops caudomaculatus*
	Caridina japonica
	Otocinclus sp.

DATA

Date / July, 2002
Aquarium / W35 x D18 x H18 (in)
Lighting / NA Lamp 32W x 6 units, turned on for 10 hours
Filter / Super Jet Filter ES-600, Bio Cube 20, Anthracite
Substrate / Aqua Soil Amazonia, Power Sand Special M, Bacter 100, Clear Super, Penac W for Aquarium, Penac P
CO₂ / Pollen Glass Beetle 30, 4 bubbles per second via CO₂ Beetle Counter
Aeration / 14 hours after the light is turned off using Lily Pipe P-4
Additives / Brighty K; Green Brighty STEP 2

Water Change / 1/3 once a week
Water Quality / Temperature 77°F; pH 7.0; TH 20mg/l
Aquatic Plants / Fontinalis antipyretica
Ludwigia arcuata
Anubias barteri var. nana
Rotala rotundifolia (green)
Ludwigia peruensis
Ludwigia repens
Rotala nanjean
Ludwigia arcuata

Animals / Hyphessobrycon haraldschultzi
Hemigrammus pulcher
Thayeria obliqua
Caridina japonica
Otocinclus sp.

DATA

Date	September, 2004
Aquarium	W71 x D47 x H24 (in)
Lighting	NAMH-150W/NA Lamp Twin 36W x 2 units (Grand Solar I) x 6 units, turned on for 10 hours
Filter	Filter Sump, Bio Rio
Substrate	Aqua Soil Amazonia, Bright Sand, Power Sand Special L, Bacter 100, Clear Super, Penac W for Aquarium, Penac P, Tourmaline BC
CO₂	Injected in the inflow Pipe, 10 bubbles per second via CO₂ Beetle Counter x 2 units
Additives	Brighty K; Green Gain; ECA
Water Change	1/3 twice a week
Water Quality	Temperature 75°F; pH 6.8; TH 10mg/l
Aquatic Plants	*Nesaea pedicellata*
	Rotala rotundifolia (green)
	Polygonum sp. "pink"
	Eusteralis sp.
	Hygrophila polysperma
	Ludwigia peruensis
	Hygrophila angustifolia
	Microsorum sp.
	Cryptocoryne albida
	Cryptocoryne wendtii (Mi Oya)
	Cryptocoryne lucens
	Fontinalis antipyretica
Animals	*Puntius denisoni*
	Trigonostigma heteromorpha
	Rasbora einthovenii
	Puntius nigrofasciatus
	Sphaerichthys osphromenoides
	Trichogaster leeri
	Otocinclus sp.
	Caridina japonica

DATA
Date	October, 2004
Aquarium	W47 x D18 x H24 (in)
Lighting	NAMH-150W (Solar I) x 2 units, turned on for 10 hours
Filter	Super Jet Filter ES-1200, Bio Rio M, NA Carbon
Substrate	Aqua Soil Amazonia, Power Sand Special L, Bacter 100, Clear Super, Tourmaline BC, Penac W for Aquarium, Penac P
CO₂	Pollen Glass Beetle 50, 5 bubbles per second via CO₂ Beetle Counter
Aeration	14 hours after the light is turned off using Lily Pipe P-6
Additives	Brighty K; Green Brighty STEP 2; Green Gain
Water Change	1/3 once a week
Water Quality	Temperature 77°F; pH 7.0; TH 50mg/l
Aquatic Plants	*Cryptocoryne balansae*
	Cryptocoryne petchii
	Crinum calamistratum

Isoetes japonica
Fontinalis antipyretica
Lilaeopsis novae-zelandiae
Microsorum sp.
Cyperus helferi

Animals *Danio choprai*
Puntius narayani
Oreichtys sp.
Caridina japonica
Otocinclus sp.

DATA

Date	October, 2004
Aquarium	W47 x D18 x H24 (in)
Lighting	NAMH-150W (Solar I) x 2 units, turned on for 10 hours
Filter	Super Jet Filter ES-1200, Bio Rio M, NA Carbon
Substrate	Aqua Soil Amazonia, Bright Sand, Power Sand Special L, Bacter 100, Clear Super, Tourmaline BC, Penac W for Aquarium, Penac P
CO_2	Pollen Glass Beetle 50, 4 bubbles per second via CO_2 Beetle Counter
Aeration	14 hours after the light is turned off using Lily Pipe P-4
Additives	Brighty K; Green Brighty STEP 2; Green Gain
Water Change	1/3 once a week
Water Quality	Temperature 77°F; pH 7.2; TH 50mg/l

Aquatic Plants / *Bolbitis heudelotii*
Rotala nanjean
Rotala rotundifolia (Green)
Rotala sp.
Microsorum sp.
Cyperus helferi
Polygonum sp. "pink"
Isoetes japonica
Eusteralis sp.
Fontinalis antipyretica
Hydrocotyle maritima

Animals / *Thayeria obliqua*
Hemigrammus pulcher   *Nannostomus trifasciatus*
Ladigesia roloffi   *Caridina japonica*
Inpaichthys kerri   *Otocinclus* sp.

TAKASHI AMANO
NATURE AQUARIUM
COMPLETE WORKS

2005-2009

DATA
Date　　　　／July, 2005
Aquarium　　／W83 x D29.5 x H29.5 (in)
Lighting　　　／NAMH-150W/NA Lamp 36W Twin x 2 units (Grand Solar I) x 3 units,
　　　　　　　turned on for 10 hours
Filter　　　　／Super Jet Filter ES-2400 x 2 units, Bio Rio, NA Carbon
Substrate　　／Aqua Soil Amazonia, Power Sand Special L, Bacter 100, Clear Super,
　　　　　　　Penac W for Aquarium, Penac P
CO₂　　　　　／Direct injection in the inflow filter pipe, 4 bubbles per second via
　　　　　　　CO₂ Beetle Counter x 2 units
Aeration　　　／14 hours after the light is turned off using
　　　　　　　Pollen Glass Beetle 50 for Air
Additives　　／Brighty K; Green Brighty STEP 2; Green Gain; Green Bacter; ECA
Water Change／1/4 once a week
Water Quality／Temperature 77°F; pH 7.0; TH 10mg/l

Aquatic Plants／*Echinodorus tenellus*
Glossostigma elatinoides
Anubias barteri var. *nana*
Bolbitis heudelotii
Microsorum sp.
Hygrophila polysperma
Hygrophila stricta sp.
Rotala rotundifolia (green)
Rotala sp.
Rotala nanjean
Rotala macrandra sp.
Ludwigia arcuata
Ludwigia glandulosa
Alternanthera reineckii

Echinodorus uruguaiensis
Cryptocoryne wendtii (green)
Cryptocoryne pontederifolia
Cyperus helferi
Isoetes japonica
Fontinalis antipyretica
Animals／*Paracheirodon axelrodi*
Hyphessobrycon pyrhonotus
Hyphessobrycon herbertaxelrodi
Hyphessobrycon megalopterus
Hyphessobrycon roseus
Otocinclus sp.
Crossocheilus siamensis
Caridina japonica

To Photograph Every Tree and Blade of Grass Faithfully

I initially used to create layouts in an aquarium while I was taking landscape photographs. Although I was not taking landscape photographs to create a layout, consequently they served as useful references for a layout. On the contrary, I take a landscape photograph nowadays using my experience gained in creating layouts and finding the beauty of nature from my own point of view. Although I did not realize clearly that an ecosystem existed in a landscape when I was younger, I came to appreciate it while I created numerous Nature Aquarium layouts. A tiny ecosystem that aquatic plants, fish, and microorganisms produce together flourishes in a beautiful aquascape. Likewise, there is an ecosystem

always thriving in a beautiful landscape.

I have been taking landscape photographs following my principle of photographing every tree and blade of grass faithfully. Unlike other landscape photographers, I get inspired by the details of nature, such as the vitality of plants, the powerfulness of rocks, and fish swimming in pristine water, and I take photographs from a totally different point of view. Although not visible, there exist insects, birds, and amphibians. I want to take a photograph that enables viewers to sense the existence of such living creatures. This is meaningful only because I use a large format film that can record nature faithfully. Someone told me that he can decipher the type of plants in my landscape photographs. I think that it is only

possible because I take pictures with details, using the large format films.

Many living creatures have disappeared from today's natural landscape. Let's say someone has taken a photograph of the same landscape as it looked 50 years ago, using large format film. If you look at the photograph with a magnifying lens, you will be stunned at the sight. You will find many different living creatures that existed there. Things have changed so drastically in a mere 50 years. I want to take a photograph of a living landscape like the one that existed in the past instead of a landscape destroyed by civilization. If there is a photograph that has recorded nature and its ecosystems faithfully just the way they were, I believe that it

will be able to provide great clues when someone tries to revive the environment 100 years from now. This is why I insist on large format films in today's era of digital cameras.

Because of the time line, we need this kind of thinking. So I established the International Environment Photographers Association in May 2009. Although artistic photography is great, I would like to take photographs that record natural ecosystems faithfully and make them available to as many people as possible. Whether it is a landscape photograph or an aquascape photograph, people are moved by something that is truly beautiful. I believe that such an

DATA

Date	May, 2005
Aquarium	W24 x D12 x H14 (in)
Lighting	NA Lamp 20W x 4 units, turned on for 10 hours
Filter	Super Jet Filter ES-600, Bio Rio, NA Carbon
Substrate	Aqua Soil Amazonia, Power Sand Special S, Bacter 100, Clear Super, Tourmaline BC, Penac W for Aquarium, Penac P
CO₂	Pollen Glass, 3 bubbles per second via CO₂ Bubble Counter
Aeration	14 hours after the light is turned off using Lily Pipe P-2
Additives	Brighty K; Green Brighty STEP 2; Green Brighty Special LIGHTS
Water Change	1/3 once a week
Water Quality	Temperature 79°F; pH 6.8; TH 10mg/l
Aquatic Plants	*Hemianthus callitrichoides* "Cuba"
	Riccia fluitans
	Eleocharis vivipara
Animals	*Danio choprae*
	Otocinclus sp.
	Crossocheilus siamensis
	Caridina japonica

DATA

Date	May, 2005
Aquarium	W24 x D12 x H18 (in)
Lighting	NA Lamp 20W x 4 units, turned on for 10 hours
Filter	Super Jet Filter ES-600, Bio Rio, NA Carbon
Substrate	Aqua Soil Amazonia, Power Sand Special S, Bacter 100, Clear Super, Tourmaline BC, Penac W for Aquarium, Penac P
CO₂	Pollen Glass, 3 bubbles per second via CO₂ Bubble Counter
Aeration	14 hours after the light is turned off using Lily Pipe P-2
Additives	Brighty K; Green Brighty STEP 2; ECA
Water Change	1/3 once a week
Water Quality	Temperature 79°F; pH 6.8; TH 20mg/l
Aquatic Plants	*Eleocharis acicularis*
	Hemianthus callitrichoides "Cuba"
Animals	*Hemigrammus armstrongi*
	Otocinclus sp.
	Crossocheilus siamensis
	Caridina japonica

DATA

Date	February, 2005
Aquarium	W35 x D18 x H18 (in)
Lighting	NA Lamp 32W x 6 units
Filter	Super Jet Filter ES-600
Substrate	Aqua Soil Amazonia, Power Sand Special M, Bacter 100, Clear Super, Tourmaline BC, Penac W for Aquarium, Penac P
CO_2	Pollen Glass Beetle 30, 3 bubbles per second via CO_2 Beetle Counter
Aeration	using Lily Pipe P-4
Additives	Brighty K; Green Brighty STEP 2; ECA
Water Change	1/3 once a week
Water Quality	Temperature 75°F; pH 6.8; TH 10mg/l

Aquatic Plants	*Riccia fluitans*
	Glossostigma elatinoides
	Echinodorus tenellus
	Fontinalis antipyretica
	Cryptocoryne wendtii (green)
	Vallisneria nana
Animals	*Trigonostigma espei*
	Caridina japonica
	Otocinclus sp.

DATA

Date	/ August, 2005
Aquarium	/ W71 x D24 x H24 (in)
Lighting	/ NAMH-150W (Solar I) x 3 units, turned on for 10 hours
Filter	/ Super Jet Filter ES-2400, Bio Rio
Substrate	/ Aqua Soil Amazonia, Power Sand Special L, Bacter 100, Clear Super,
	Tourmaline BC, Penac W for Aquarium, Penac P
CO₂	/ Pollen Glass Beetle 50, 6 bubbles per second via CO₂ Beetle Counter
Aeration	/ Using Lily Pipe P-6
Additives	/ Brighty K; Green Brighty STEP 2; ECA; Green Gain
Water Change	/ 1/3 once a week

Water Quality	/ Temperature 75°F; pH 6.8; TH 50mg/l
Aquatic Plants	/ *Riccia fluitans*
	Glossostigma elatinoides
Animals	/ *Paracheirodon simulans*
	Caridina japonica
	Crossocheilus siamensis
	Otocinclus sp.

Continually Evolving Cube Garden Aquariums

An aquarium is essential for creating Nature Aquarium layouts. However, older aquariums were meant for keeping fish, and therefore they had a number of problems for displaying aquascapes beautifully. Thick, noticeable silicone seams and stainless steel or plastic frames of a glass aquarium were impediments, and the bluish green tint of the glass was noticeable as well. Although acrylic aquariums were not tinted and didn't have the problem of seams, they had tendencies to get fine scratches easily and lose

clarity quickly. Although I have used these types of commercially available aquariums in the early days of Nature Aquarium, my desire to show off an aquascape that I created more attractively grew stronger with time, and eventually I decided to produce the ideal aquarium myself.

Thus the first Cube Garden (the current Cube Garden Superior) was born. This aquarium was produced by melting and joining sheets of almost colorless lab grade plate glass. It was an all glass aquarium without silicone seams and frames. However, its

special material and production method limited the size to a 2-foot-aquarium, and its price was exceptionally high as well. Therefore, I used this type to created layouts designed for a tiny nano aquarium up to a 2-foot-aquarium, but it was not the type of product that would become widely popular. Soon the current Cube Garden aquariums were developed because these ideal glass aquariums could be produced in larger sizes at lower prices that were more attractive to the general public. By joining sheets of highly clear plate glass together with the smallest amount of

silicone, the inside of an aquarium looks brighter and its seams appear less noticeable. An Iwagumi layout created in the image of vast grassland can be viewed clearly without anything blocking the wide field of view, and its appeal can be conveyed without obstruction. At present, the Mist Type, with its frosted rear glass, and the Mist R Type, with its side and rear panels consolidated seamlessly into a curved glass sheet, are also available. Cube Garden aquariums continue to evolve to present an aquascape more attractively.

1: In the case of a split pattern substrate that uses Aqua Soil and Cosmetic Sand, a wide cardboard strip is placed along the dividing line and temporarily secured in place with small rocks. In this layout, I decided to use a pattern that divides the space in the aquarium into the left and right sides in a 3:2 proportion, with cosmetic sand stretching toward the rear of the aquarium between the two sides. A layout like this appears more pleasing to the eye if the left and right sides are not divided evenly and if the balance of the two sides is tipped toward one side. This balance is so called Golden Ratio (1:1.618) and serves as a useful reference for creating a layout as well.

2: Cosmetic sand was placed in the front of the cardboard strip and Aqua Soil Amazonia was placed behind the strip. Since aquatic plants are not planted in the cosmetic sand, the sand does not need to be too deep. A thin layer of sand is pleasing to the eye, too. The most important thing to keep in mind here is the height of the cosmetic sand and Aqua Soil at the cardboard boundary, which must be even. Otherwise, the boundary line will be spoiled when the cardboard is pulled out. After the substrate of cosmetic sand and Aqua Soil is laid, the heights of the two must be carefully checked to make sure that they are even from the sides of the aquarium.

5: After all of the rocks are placed and the overall balance of the Iwagumi layout is checked, aquatic plants will be planted next. In a layout with cosmetic sand, the soil must be retained at the boundary of the cosmetic sand and Aqua Soil. Aqua Soil will tend to flow out over the cosmetic sand and make the water maintenance difficult unless soil retainers are placed. Small stones to which *Riccia* was secured with Riccia Line were placed on the boundary of the cosmetic sand and Aqua Soil at this point. The rocks

6: Water was added to the aquarium as in the photograph in order to barely submerge the Aqua Soil which forms an area to plant short aquatic plants. The balance of the planting spaces of individual aquatic plants was checked using bamboo sticks. A method like this is helpful for beginners since the balance of planting spaces can be checked easily with it. The use of bamboo sticks is also convenient for estimating the necessary volumes of individual aquatic plants when making a planting plan.

: Since the substrate area was divided into the 3:2 proportions, the rocks should also be arranged keep-g this proportion in mind. The presence of an Oyaishi (main stone) is the most important thing in agumi, and therefore the Oyaishi must be selected carefully. Its size must be appropriate to the size of e aquarium and the shape needs to be examined closely. It is even better if the rock has a regal ppearance as well. After the Oyaishi is chosen, the Fukuishi (secondary stone) and Soeishi ccompanying/subordinate stone) should be selected to match the atmosphere of the Oyaishi. Doing so eates a sense of unity in the overall Iwagumi. In this layout, Manten stone was placed toward the left de of the aquarium as the Oyaishi by carefully examining its orientation and tilt.

4: Smaller rocks were selected and arranged on the right side as accompanying rocks to the Oyaishi or the left side. Two groupings of three rocks consisting of Oyaishi, Fukuishi, and Soeishi were examined fo each of the left and right sides. Such an Iwagumi made of two groups of rocks is a relatively difficul arrangement since the balance of the two groups must also be kept in mind. Although it is important to find a place where rocks would look their best, their placement must be carefully evaluated since strengt and forcefulness can be expressed with the angle of a rock. Rocks should be placed one by one by checking the balance of each rock from a horizontal position as each are placed in a layout.

: *Glossostigma* was planted in the area in front of the rocks using bamboo sticks as a guide. *Glossostigma,* hich spreads like a carpet, can be expected to have the effect of retaining the soil as well. Next, *hinodorus tenellus* was planted between rocks. This plant works to tie the rocks together to produce the ontinuity among the Iwagumi arrangements. Lastly, hair grass was planted behind the Iwagumi, and *eocharis vivipara* was planted further behind them.

8: After gently adding dechlorinated tap water to the aquarium, taller plants, such as *E. vivipara* were gently coaxed upright using tweezers since they tend to lie down in a tangled up condition. After install-ing Lily Pipes for the filter and the CO_2 injection equipment as shown in the photograph, a Drop Checke was added on the opposite side of the CO_2 diffuser. Since the demand of CO_2 is high in a layout with *Riccia*, CO_2 should be monitored for proper injection volume using the Drop Checker to avoid CO_2

DATA

Date	/ July, 2005	Water Quality	/ Temperature 77°F; pH 6.8; TH 10mg/l
Aquarium	/ W35 x D18 x H18 (in)	Aquatic Plants	/ *Glossostigma elatinoides*
Lighting	/ NAG-150W (Solar I) Green x 1 units, turned on for 10 hours		*Riccia fluitans*
Filter	/ Super Jet Filter ES-600, Bio Cube, Anthracite		*Eleocharis acicularis*
Substrate	/ Aqua Soil Amazonia, Bright Sand, Power Sand Special M,		*Eleocharis vivipara*
	Bacter 100, Clear Super, Tourmaline BC,		*Echinodorus tenellus*
	Penac W for Aquarium, Penac P	Animals	/ *Hyphessobrycon herbertaxelrodi*
CO₂	/ Pollen Glass Beetle 30,		*Crossocheilus siamensis*
	3 bubbles per second via CO₂ Beetle Counter		*Otocinclus* sp.
Aeration	/ 14 hours after the light is turned off using Lily Pipe P-4		*Caridina japonica*
Additives	/ Brighty K; Green Brighty STEP 2		
Water Change	/ 1/3 once a week		

DATA

Date	/March, 2005
Aquarium	/W35 x D18 x H18 (in)
Lighting	/NA Lamp 32W x 6 units, turned on for 10 hours
Filter	/Super Jet Filter ES-600, Bio Rio, NA Carbon
Substrate	/Aqua Soil Amazonia, Bright Sand, Power Sand Special M,
	Bacter 100, Clear Super, Tourmaline BC,
	Penac W for Aquarium, Penac P
CO₂	/Pollen Glass Beetle 40,
	3 bubbles per second via CO₂ Beetle Counter
Aeration	/14 hours after the light is turned off using Lily Pipe P-4
Additives	/Brighty K; Green Brighty STEP 2
Water Change	/1/3 once a week
Water Quality	/Temperature 79°F; pH 7.0; TH 30mg/l

Aquatic Plants	/Vallisneria nana
	Cryptocoryne wendtii (green)
	Cryptocoryne wendtii (brown)
	Fontinalis antipyretica
	Bolbitis heudelotii
Animals	/Prionobrama filigere
	Otocinclus sp.
	Caridina japonica

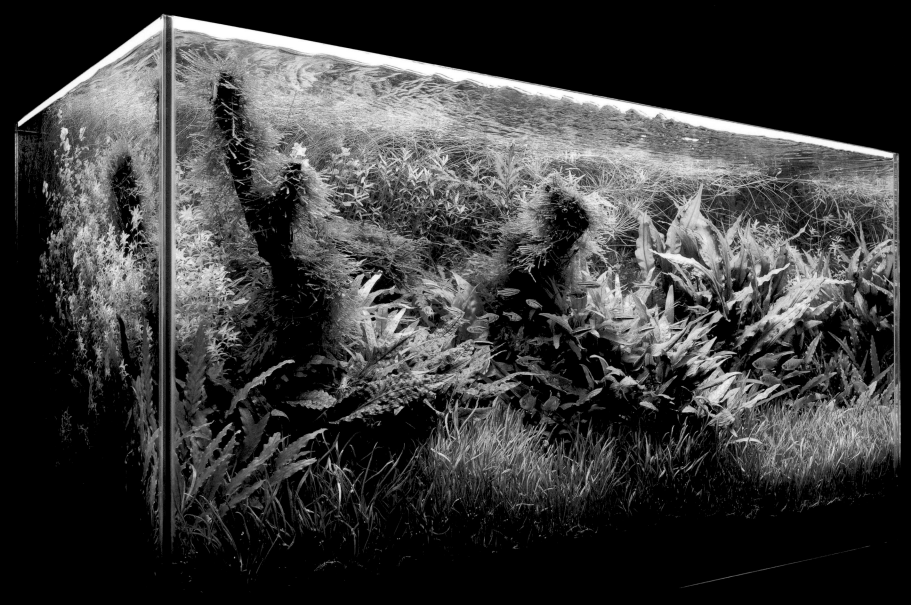

DATA

Date	September, 2005
Aquarium	W35 x D18 x H18 (in)
Lighting	NAG-150W Green/NA Lamp 36W Twin x 2 units (Grand Solar I), turned on for 10 hours
Filter	Super Jet Filter ES-600, Bio Rio, NA Carbon
Substrate	Aqua Soil Amazonia, Power Sand Special M, Bacter 100, Clear Super, Tourmaline BC, Penac W for Aquarium, Penac P

CO₂	Pollen Glass Beetle 30, 3 bubbles per second via CO₂ Beetle Counter
Aeration	14 hours after the light is turned off using Lily Pipe P-4
Additives	Brighty K; Green Brighty STEP 2
Water Change	1/3 once a week
Water Quality	Temperature 77°F; pH 6.8; TH 10mg/l
Aquatic Plants	*Cryptocoryne petchii*
	Cryptocoryne lucens
	Cryptocoryne wendtii (**Mi Oya**)
	Fontinalis antipyretica
	Cryptocoryne wendtii (**green**)

	Lilaeopsis novae-zelandiae
	Eusteralis stellata
	Hemianthus micranthemoides
	Micranthemum unbrosum
	Rotala rotundifolia
	Eleocharis vivipara
Animals	*Trigonostigma espei*
	Rasbora borapetensis
	Hyphessobrycon rosaceus var.
	Hyphessobrycon herbertaxelrodi
	Caridina japonica
	Otocinclus sp.

ATA

ate	May, 2005
quarium	W35 x D18 x H18 (in)
ghting	NAG-150W Green/NA Lamp 36W Twin x 2 units
	(Grand Solar I), turned on for 10 hours
ilter	Super Jet Filter ES-600, Bio Cube 20, Anthracite
ubstrate	Aqua Soil Amazonia, Power Sand Special M, Bacter 100,
	Clear Super, Tourmaline BC, Penac W for Aquarium, Penac P
O₂	Pollen Glass Beetle 30,
	3 bubbles per second via CO_2 Beetle Counter
eration	14 hours after the light is turned off using Lily Pipe P-4
dditives	Brighty K; Green Brighty STEP 2; Green Gain
ater Change	1/3 once a week
ater Quality	Temperature 75°F; pH 6.8; TH 20mg/l
quatic Plants	*Rotala rotundifolia*
	Rotala macrandra **sp.**

Rotala rotundifolia **(green)**
Rotala **sp.**
Rotala macrandra
Eusteralis **sp.**
Micranthemum unbrosum
Ludwigia arcuata
Eleocharis vivipara
Riccia fluitans
Glossostigma elatinoides
Echinodorus tenellus
Fontinalis antipyretica
Microsorum **sp.**
Bolbitis heudelotii
Anubias barteri var. nana **(narrow)**
Cryptocoryne pontederifolia

Cryptocoryne wendtii **(green)**
Cryptocoryne wendtii **(Mi Oya)**
Animals *Thayeria boehlkei*
Hemigrammus pulcher
Hyphessobrycon sweglesi
Nematobrycon palmeri
Caridina japonica
Crossocheilus siamensis
Otocinclus **sp.**

1 : The substrate of cosmetic sand and Aqua Soil was prepared in a 3:2 balance from left to right in the 71 x 24 x 24 inches aquarium shown in this photograph. Power Sand L, which provides the nutrients in the substrate, was placed only in the planting section made of Aqua Soil. When creating planting spaces in the left and right sides of an aquarium, care must be taken not to make the areas symmetrical in proportion.

The fine-grained, pure white sand of the Negro River in the Amazon was used as cosmetic sand in this layout.

2 : Branchy driftwood was arranged at the boundary of cosmetic sand and Aqua Soil. The volumes of driftwood in the left and right sides were changed according to the ratio of Aqua Soil laid in the left and right sides of the aquarium. Since driftwood pieces were arranged in a way so that their tips extended into the empty space, each piece was selected carefully by closely examining the shape of the tips. Because the balance between the empty space in the center over the cosmetic sand that stretches toward the rear of the aquarium and the tips of the driftwood becomes the key in this layout composition, the driftwood was arranged by carefully checking the directions and angles of the individual branches. When using a large number of driftwood branches as in this layout, careful attention

3: When this many dark colored driftwood pieces are used in a layout, the color of their surfaces tends to appear too strong. Therefore, I wrapped willow moss over the tips and various places of the driftwood using Moss Cotton. Doing so not only softens the strong contrast of colors, but it also renders a mossy, natural appearance. Various sized rocks that were wrapped with willow moss using Riccia Line were placed tightly over the boundary as soil retainers so as not to create a gap. This completed the foundation for a layout.

4: Since I wanted to display the line of driftwood attractively in this layout, I chose to plant long, fine leaved aquatic plants primarily, rather than using colorful stem plants in the background. Since the layout will appear monotonous with only a single type of plant, I planted *Echinodorus angustifolius*, *Isoetes japonica*, *Eleocharis vivipara*, and *Crinum calamistratum* together. Lastly, I attached *Bolbitis* in various parts of the driftwood with Wood Tight to create an atmosphere that relates to Wabi-Sabi (Japanese world view or aesthetic centered on the acceptance of transience).
*The finished aquascape is shown in the next page.

DATA
Date / October, 2005
Aquarium / W71 x D24 x H24 (in)
Lighting / NAG-150W Green (Solar I) x 3 units, turned on for 10 hours
Filter / Super Jet Filter ES-2400, Bio Rio, NA Carbon
Substrate / Aqua Soil Amazonia, Rio Negro Sand,
    Power Sand Special L, Bacter 100, Clear Super,
    Tourmaline BC, Penac W for Aquarium, Penac P
CO₂ / Pollen Glass Beetle 50,
    6 bubbles per second via CO₂ Beetle Counter
Aeration / 14 hours after the light is turned off using Lily Pipe P-6
Additives / Brighty K; Green Brighty STEP 2

Water Change / 1/3 once a week
Water Quality / Temperature 75°F; pH 6.8; TH 20mg/l
Aquatic Plants / *Rotala rotundifolia*
    Rotala macrandra sp.
    Echinodrus angustifolia
    Crinum calamistratum
    Eleocharis vivipara
    Vallisneria nana
    Isoetes japonica
    Bolbitis heudelotii
    Fontinalis antipyretica

Animals / *Hemigrammus rodwayi*
    Hemigrammopetersius caudalis
    Moenkhausia pittieri
    Crossocheilus siamensis
    Otocinclus sp.
    Caridina japonica

Maintaining an Aquascape for a Long Period of Time

I have had the idea of maintaining an aquascape for an extended period of time ever since I started creating aquatic plant layouts. I also work with biotopes and natural bonsai, both of which are maintained over the span of a few hundred years. They have the flavors of fine, old things that have been nurtured by time. I aim to create things that are maintained for a long time, and Nature Aquarium is no exception. It is difficult to keep up frequent maintenance work for many years. The secret for maintaining a layout over a long period of time is to produce a layout that does not require much maintenance work. For example, it is necessary to use slow growing

mosses and plants in the family of ferns that do not require frequent trimming, and it is also important to use a design that is easy to maintain. The main reason an aquascape deteriorates over time is the overgrowth of aquatic plants. To keep an aquascape from declining, fast growing stem plants in particular should be decisively trimmed short. After a number of trimmings, the stem plants need to be rejuvenated by cutting off the old parts and planting young tips at the appropriate time. This keeps stems from aging. Old fern leaves should be cut off and mosses that are attached to driftwood should be trimmed before they get too thick. In either case, the key to success is to cut decisively. Although this aquascape has been

maintained over six years, its aquatic plants have been maintained by trimming and replanting the tops, and the plants have never been replaced since the beginning. *Bolbitis* extended emersed grown leaves above the water surface and *Crinum* bloomed with big flowers many times. Diamond tetra and emperor tetra spawned and the new generation replaced the old generation naturally. One thing that became clear during the long term maintenance was the difficulty of maintaining the Rio Negro Sand, which was used as cosmetic sand. Not only were the waste materials of shrimp and fish and the small particles of Aqua Soil highly noticeable on the pure white sand, but the sand also turned dark and dingy from algae growing on the

surface or bacteria multiplying on it over time. Therefore, it became necessary to suction out surface dirt frequently as well as turn the sand over periodically. Although this type of maintenance is possible in the Gallery where ADA staff can take care of them frequently, it is a lot of work for ordinary hobbyists who are busy with their own work. Also in the case of white sand, the sand limits the expression of the passage of time by its very white appearance. Therefore, in later aquascapes I've come to use a type of cosmetic sand that is easier to care for from the long term maintenance standpoint.

Recommendations for an Always Presentable Aquascape

One of the reasons why I established Nature Aquarium Gallery was to demonstrate the long term maintenance of an aquascape. Many of the readers of aquarium magazines know Nature Aquarium only through photographs and articles. Since aquascape photographs are taken generally when all of the aquatic plants are grown and look beautiful, it was difficult to convey the information on both the growing process of aquatic plants after the initial planting and how the aquascape is maintained for a long time after the photo shoot.

In the gallery, aquascapes in various stages are on display, including those that are just created. An aquascape in the early stages, right after setting up, can give you a useful reference on the ratio of the foreground and background areas that are separated by the middle ground, the planting density of each aquatic plant, and the way willow moss is wrapped on driftwood. Since aquatic plants

DATA

Date	/September, 2006	Aquatic Plants	/*Isoetes japonica*
Aquarium	/W47 x D18 x H24 (in)		*Eleocharis vivipara*
Lighting	/NAMH-150W (Solar I) x 2 units, turned on for 10 hours		*Echinodorus angstifolia*
Filter	/Super Jet Filter ES-1200, Bio Rio		*Vallisneria nana*
Substrate	/Aqua Soil Amazonia, Nile Sand, Power Sand Special L,		*Cryptocoryne wendtii* (green)
	Bacter 100, Clear Super, Tourmaline BC,		*Cryptocoryne wendtii* (Tropica)
	Penac W for Aquarium, Penac P		*Microsorum* sp.
CO₂	/Pollen Glass Beetle 50,		*Fontinalis antipyretica*
	3 bubbles per second via CO₂ Beetle Counter	Animals	/*Rasbora vaterifloris*
Aeration	/14 hours after the light is turned off using Lily Pipe P-4		*Trigonostigma espei*
Additives	/Brighty K; Green Brighty STEP 2; Green Gain		*Caridina japonica*
Water Change	/1/3 once a week		*Crossocheilus siamensis*
Water Quality	/Temperature 79°F; pH 7.0; TH 30mg/l		*Otocinclus* sp.

are trimmed as they start growing, you can see the location of the cuts on stem plants, the slant of the trimmed bushes, and the trimming method for undergrowth. The biggest reason for the decline of a layout is the overgrown aquatic plants filling up all the space in the aquarium. By then the stems and leaves on the lower part of the plants have melted and the layout can no longer be revived, even with trimming. Therefore, we try to keep plants trimmed somewhat early in the gallery.

However, the cut surfaces of aquatic plants look unattractive right after trimming since the beautiful parts of the plants are lost temporarily. This tendency is particularly obvious in layouts that are created primarily with stem plants. So, I considered a layout method in which a layout does not appear too unsightly right after stem plants are trimmed. First, cosmetic sand is placed in the foreground. This eliminates the necessity of trimming, thereby making maintenance easier, and adjusts the brightness of the overall

aquascape. Then, the middle ground is built up somewhat high with driftwood, to which ferns and willow moss are attached. Since ferns and willow moss grow relatively slowly, frequent trimming is not necessary as in the case of stem plants. An aquascape that is always presentable is complete when stem plants are planted in the background since the appearance of the foreground and the middle ground stays the same right after trimming.

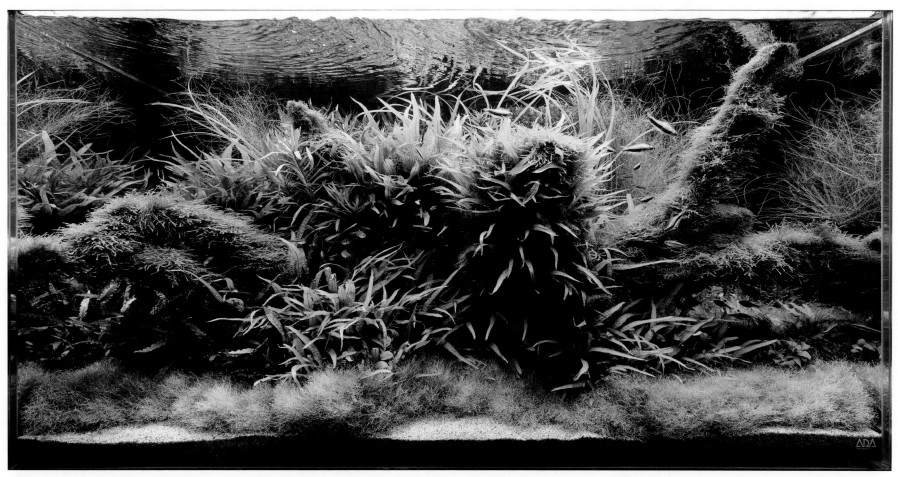

DATA

Date	/ September, 2006	Aquatic Plants	/ *Ludwigia* sp."Cuba"	Animals	/ *Paracheirodon innesi*
Aquarium	/ W47 x D18 x H24 (in)		*Nesaea pedicellata*		*Hyphessobrycon megalopterus*
Lighting	/ NAMH-150W (Solar I) x 2 units, turned on for 10 hours		*Rotala rotundifolia*		*Hyphessobrycon heterorhabdus*
Filter	/ Super Jet Filter ES-1200, Bio Rio		*Cyperus helferi*		*Aphyocharax rathbuni*
Substrate	/ Aqua Soil Amazonia, Sarawak Sand, Power Sand Special L,		*Eleocharis vivipara*		*Nematobrycon palmeri*
	Bacter 100, Clear Super, Tourmaline BC,		*Cryptocoryne petchii*		*Caridina japonica*
	Penac W for Aquarium, Penac P		*Cryptocoryne wendtii* (Mi Oya)		*Crossocheilus siamensis*
CO₂	/ Pollen Glass Beetle 50,		*Cryptocoryne pontederifolia*		*Otocinclus* sp.
	4 bubbles per second via CO₂ Beetle Counter		*Cryptocoryne lucens*		
Aeration	/ 14 hours after the light is turned off using Lily Pipe P-6		*Riccia fluitans*		
Additives	/ Brighty K; Green Brighty STEP 2; Green Gain		*Microsorum* sp.		
Water Change	/ 1/3 once a week		*Fontinalis antipyretica*		
Water Quality	/ Temperature 79°F; pH 7.0; TH 20mg/l				

DATA

Date	October, 2006	Water Quality	Temperature 77°F; pH 7.0; TH 20mg/l		*Isoetes japonica*
Aquarium	W35 x D18 x H18 (in)	Aquatic Plants	*Riccia fluitans*		*Microsorum* sp.
Lighting	NAMH-150W (Solar I) x 1.5 units, turned on for 10 hours		*Glossostigma elatinoides*		*Fontinalis antipyretica*
Filter	Super Jet Filter ES-1200, Bio Rio, NA Carbon		*Echinodorus tenellus*	Animals	*Hemigrammus armstrongi*
Substrate	Aqua Soil Amazonia, Power Sand Special L, Bacter 100,		*Echinodorus latifolius*		*Ladigesia roloffi*
	Clear Super, Tourmaline BC, Penac W for Aquarium, Penac P		*Echinodorus angustifolia*		*Microgeophagus ramirezi*
CO₂	Pollen Glass Large 30,		*Rotala* **sp.**		*Caridina japonica*
	4 bubbles per second via CO₂ Beetle Counter		*Myriophyllum mattogrossense* **(green)**		*Otocinclus* **sp.**
Aeration	14 hours after the light is turned off using Lily Pipe P-4		*Ludwigia arcuata*		
Additives	Brighty K; Green Brighty STEP 2; ECA		*Rotala nanjean*		
Water Change	1/3 once a week		*Rotala rotundifolia*		

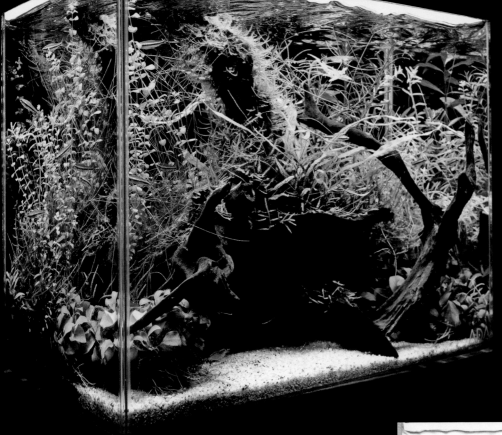

DATA
Date   September, 2006
Aquarium   W12 x D7 x H9.5 (in)
Lighting   Solar Mini 27W Twin, turned on for 10 hours
Filter   External Filter, NA Carbon
Substrate   Bright Sand
CO₂   Pollen Glass Mini,
                1 bubble per every 3 seconds via CO₂ Bubble Counter
Additives   Brighty K; Green Brighty STEP 2
Water Change   1/3 once a week
Water Quality   Temperature 77°F; pH 7.0; TH 20mg/l
Aquatic Plants Wabi Kusa Stemmed Plants MIX
                Microsorum sp.
                Anubias barteri var. *nana* (petit)
                Fontinalis antipyretica
Animals   *Nannostomus beckfordi*
                Caridina japonica

DATA
Date   September, 2006
Aquarium   W14 x D9 x H10 (in)
Lighting   Solar Mini 27W Twin, turned on for 10 hours
Filter   External Filter, NA Carbon
Substrate   Aqua Soil Amazonia Powder, Bacter 100, Clear Super,
                Tourmaline BC, Penac W for Aquarium, Penac P
CO₂   Pollen Glass Mini,
                1 bubble per every 2 seconds via CO₂ Bubble Counter
Additives   Brighty K; Green Brighty STEP 2
Water Change   1/3 once a week
Water Quality   Temperature 77°F; pH 7.0; TH 20mg/l
Aquatic Plants *Hemianthus callitrichoides* "Cuba"
                Glossostigma elatinoides
                Riccia fluitans
Animals   *Paracheirodon simulans*
                Caridina japonica

DATA	
Date	February, 2005
Aquarium	W71 x D24 x H24 (in)
Lighting	NA Lamp 20W x 12 units
Filter	Super Jet Filter ES-2400, Bio Rio
Substrate	Aqua Soil Amazonia, Power Sand Special L, Bacter 100,
	Clear Super, Tourmaline BC, Penac W for Aquarium, Penac P
CO₂	Pollen Glass Beetle 50,
	5 bubbles per second via CO₂ Beetle Counter
Aeration	14 hours after the light is turned off using Lily Pipe P-6
Additives	Brighty K; Green Brighty STEP 2

Water Change	1/3 once a week
Water Quality	Temperature 75°F; pH 6.8; TH 10mg/l
Aquatic Plants	*Cryptocoryne petchii*
	Cryptocoryne wendtii (**Mi Oya**)
	Cryptocoryne pontederifolia
	Cryptocoryne wendtii (**green**)
	Cryptocoryne wendtii var. *wendtii*
	Cryptocoryne beckettii
	Cryptocoryne balansae
	Fontinalis antipyretica

	Eleocharis acicularis
Animals	*Trigonostigma heteromorpha*
	Rasbora bankanensis
	Rasbora einthovenii
	Rasbora vaterifloris
	Rasbora caudimaculata
	Puntius kumingi
	Caridina japonica
	Otocinclus sp.

To Understand the Biology of Aquatic Plants

One comes to understand the biology of almost all aquatic plants after many years of producing Nature Aquarium layouts. This understanding extends to many aspects, such as the environment that each aquatic plant prefers, how it grows and multiplies, and the time period during which it performs photosynthesis. Although I often explain the environmental preferences of aquatic plants by dividing them into categories of heliophytic and sciophytic aquatic plants, there are variations even within each group, such as some plants that prefer slightly different light intensities and those that close their leaves depending on a time period as a result of nicti-nasty. It is necessary to modify the trimming method, the location

DATA

Date	April, 2007	Aquatic Plants	*Pogostemon sp. "Dassen"*	*Bolbitis heudelotii*
Aquarium	W24 x D12 x H14 (in)		*Myriophyllum mattogrossense* (green)	*Riccia fluitans*
Lighting	NA Lamp 36W Twin x 2 units		*Rotala nanjean*	*Fontinalis antipyretica*
Filter	Super Jet Filter ES-600, Bio Rio		*Rotala macrandra sp.*	*Eleocharis vivipara*
Substrate	Aqua Soil Amazonia, Bright Sand, Power Sand Special S,		*Ludwigia arcuata*	Animals / *Trigonostigma espei*
	Bacter 100, Clear Super, Tourmaline BC,		*Micranthemum unbrosum*	*Caridina japonica*
	Penac W for Aquarium, Penac P		*Anubias barteri var. nana* (narrow)	*Otocinclus sp.*
CO_2	Pollen Glass, 3 bubbles per second via CO_2 Bubble Counter		*Cryptocoryne petchii*	
Aeration	14 hours after the light is turned off using Lily Pipe P-2		*Cryptocoryne wendtii* (green)	
Additives	Brighty K; Green Brighty STEP 2; ECA		*Microsorum sp.*	
Water Change	1/3 once a week			
Water Quality	Temperature 75°F; pH 6.8; TH 20mg/l			

and density of the plants depending on their biological differences, and the type of substrate, lighting intensity, and maintenance method also need to be changed. When creating a layout, it would be ideal to know the biology of the particular aquatic plants to be used. Knowing that will enable us to use aquatic plants in a reasonable manner.

In a flower garden style of layout that used to be mainstream in Europe, stem plants were planted all over the aquarium and the entire layout was light-oriented. The concept of shade may not have existed. On the other hand, one of the characteristics of Nature Aquarium is to use natural materials, such as driftwood and rocks. Sciophytic plants, such as *Cryptocoryne*, which does not

require strong light, is planted or a rock is placed in an area shaded by the materials. Shade is indispensible in Nature Aquarium in order to make an aquascape appear three dimensional. Therefore, I consider it quite important to master the use of shade.

In fact, one can define Nature Aquarium as the layout method based on the biology of aquatic plants. The significance of the hierarchical structure of a layout consisting of foreground, middle ground, and background and that of the use of rocks and driftwood can be explained from that. The foreground is planted with short aquatic plants that spread horizontally with runners. The background is planted with stem plants or aquatic plants with tape-

shaped leaves

that become tall enough to reach the water surface. The middle ground is planted with medium-height aquatic plants that can hide the bottom of the plants in the background and tie the background to the foreground in height. Rocks and driftwood have the functions of not only forming the composition but also adjusting the light levels, providing places to grow for epiphytic plants, and containing aquatic plants from spreading out of bounds. Although the rules for planting aquatic plants are common practice in Nature Aquarium now, they were derived from the biology of aquatic plants.

DATA

Date	/April, 2005
Aquarium	/W35 x D18 x H24 (in)
Lighting	/NAG-150W (Solar I) Green x 2 units
Filter	/Super Jet Filter ES-1200, Bio Rio
Substrate	/Aqua Soil Amazonia, Power Sand Special L, Bacter 100,
	Clear Super, Penac W for Aquarium, Penac P
CO₂	/Pollen Glass Beetle 50,
	3 bubbles per second via CO₂ Beetle Counter
Aeration	/14 hours after the light is turned off using Lily Pipe P-4
Additives	/Brighty K; Green Brighty STEP 2
Water Change	/1/3 once a week

Water Quality	/Temperature 75ºF; pH 6.6; TH 20mg/l
Aquatic Plants	/*Lilaeopsis novae-zelandiae*
	Fontinalis antipyretica
	Cryptocoryne lucens
	Cryptocoryne wendtii (Tropica)
	Cryptocoryne wendtii (green)
	Cryptocoryne wendtii (brown)
	Cryptocoryne balansae
Animals	/*Trigonostigma heteromorpha*
	Otocinclus sp.
	Caridina japonica

DATA

Date	/ November, 2005
Aquarium	/ W47 x D18 x H18 (in)
Lighting	/ NA Lamp 20W x 12 units
Filter	/ Super Jet Filter ES-1200, Bio Rio, NA Carbon
Substrate	/ Aqua Soil Amazonia, Rio Negro Sand, Power Sand Special M, Bacter 100, Clear Super, Tourmaline BC, Penac W for Aquarium, Penac P
CO_2	/ Pollen Glass Beetle 40, 3 bubbles per second via CO_2 Beetle Counter
Aeration	/ 14 hours after the light is turned off using Lily Pipe P-4
Additives	/ Brighty K; Green Brighty STEP 2; ECA
Water Change	/ 1/3 once a week
Water Quality	/ Temperature 75°F; pH 6.8; TH 20mg/l

Aquatic Plants / *Eleocharis vivipara*
Isoetes japonica
Echinodorus angstifolia
Vallisneria nana
Cryptocoryne wendtii (green)
Cryptocoryne wendtii (Tropica)
Fontinalis antipyretica
Anubias barteri var. *nana* (narrow)
Microsorum sp.
Bolbitis heudelotii
Cryptocoryne petchii
Cryptocoryne wendtii (Mi Oya)
Cryptocoryne balansae
Blyxa auberti

Animals / *Trigonostigma hengeli*
Caridina japonica
Otocinclus sp.

DATA

		Aquatic Plants	*Eleocharis vivipara*	Animals	*Rasbora vaterifloris*
Date	February, 2005		*Echinodorus angustifolia*		*Rasbora dorsiocellata macrophthalma*
Aquarium	W35 x D18 x H18 (in)		*Cryptocoryne wendtii* (**Mi Oya**)		*Orechthys cosuatis*
Lighting	NA Lamp 32W x 6 units, turned on for 10 hours		*Cryptocoryne pontederifolia*		*Caridina japonica*
Filter	Super Jet Filter ES-600, Bio Rio, NA Carbon		*Crinum calamistratum*		*Crossocheilus siamensis*
Substrate	Aqua Soil Amazonia, Rio Negro Sand, Power Sand		*Bolbitis heudelotii*		*Otocinclus* sp.
	Special M, Bacter 100, Clear Super, Tourmaline BC,		*Riccia fluitans*		
	Penac W for Aquarium, Penac P		*Fontinalis antipyretica*		
CO₂	Pollen Glass Beetle 30,				
	3 bubbles per second via CO₂ Beetle Counter				
Aeration	14 hours after the light is turned off using Lily Pipe P-4				
Additives	Brighty K; Green Brighty STEP 2				
Water Change	1/3 once a week				

DATA

Date / April, 2007

Aquarium / W35 x D18 x H18 (in)

Lighting / NAG-150W Green/NA Lamp
36W Twin x 2 units (Grand Solar I),
turned on for 10 hours

Filter / Super Jet Filter ES-600, Bio Rio, NA Carbon

Substrate / Aqua Soil Amazonia, Power Sand Special M,
Bacter 100, Clear Super, Tourmaline BC,
Penac W for Aquarium, Penac P

CO₂ / Pollen Glass Large 30,
3 bubbles per second via CO₂ Beetle Counter

Aeration / 14 hours after the light is turned off using Lily Pipe P-4

Additives / Brighty K; Green Brighty STEP 2

Water Change / 1/3 once a week

Water Quality / Temperature 77°F; pH 6.8; TH 10mg/l

Aquatic Plants / *Lilaeopsis novae-zelandiae*
Rotala sp.
Rotala nanjean
Myriophyllum mattogrossense (green)
Ludwigia arcuata
Rotala rotundifolia

Nesaea pedicellata
Rotala rotundifolia (green)
Cryptocoryne petchii
Cryptocoryne wendtii (green)
Fontinalis antipyretica
Microsorum sp.
Anubias barteri var. *nana* (narrow)

Animals / *Hyphessobrycon sweglesi*
Nematobrycon lacortei
Nannostomus trifasciatus
Caridina japonica
Crossocheilus siamensis
Otocinclus sp.

Nature Aquarium Layout That Appeared In a Movie

"Sono toki wa kare ni yoroshiku" is a novel by Takuji Ichikawa. The story takes place in a small aquatic plant aquarium shop that is run by the main character. The author enjoys keeping an aquatic plant layout himself, and he visited the Nature Aquarium Gallery at ADA's headquarters while he was writing the story. Partly because of this relationship, when this novel was about to be made into a movie, we received a request from the producer of the movie company, Toho, to provide support for filming. They wanted to reproduce the aquatic plant aquarium shop in its entirety in the movie studio.

Although the shop's sales aquariums could be set up with aquatic plants at the studio, it was not possible to create finished layouts on site. Not only were the number of days for shooting the movie limited according to the provided schedule, they also wanted at least ten Nature Aquarium tanks set up for the inside appearance of the shop. To make this possible, the aquariums that were on display at the Nature Aquarium Gallery at ADA's headquarters in Niigata had to be brought into the studio in Tokyo. To make matters worse, the aquariums had to be transported in the dead of the winter in an insulated vehicle to maintain their temperatures. After these aquariums were delivered safely with the help of all my staff, a realistic looking aquatic plant shop was recreated in the studio and I felt quite relieved as a result. However, my work was not finished yet.

It took several days to bring the aquascapes in these aquariums back to their original, beautiful conditions since the aquatic plants were disheveled and not ready for shooting right after delivery. I was also asked to coach the principle actors, Takayuki Yamada and Masami Nagasawa, who played the role of the aquarium shop keepers, on how to use the tweezers and scissors made for aquatic plants. During rehearsals and the actual shooting, I was quite anxious and was checking the actors' performances with bated breath. During a break, I asked the actors and camera crew which aquascape they liked the most. The most popular one was this Iwagumi layout. The spacious Iwagumi layout might have been easing mounting tensions they felt during shooting with its expansive, majestic impression.

DATA

Date	September, 2006
Aquarium	W47 x D18 x H18 (in)
Lighting	NAMH-150W (Solar I) x 2 units, turned on for 10 hours
Filter	Super Jet Filter ES-1200
Substrate	Aqua Soil Amazonia, Power Sand Special M, Bacter 100, Clear Super, Tourmaline BC, Penac W for Aquarium, Penac P
CO₂	Pollen Glass Beetle 50, 4 bubbles per second via CO₂ Beetle Counter
Aeration	14 hours after the light is turned off using Lily Pipe P-4
Additives	Brighty K; Green Brighty STEP 2
Water Change	1/3 once a week
Water Quality	Temperature 75°F; pH 7.0; TH 100mg/l
Aquatic Plants	*Riccia fluitans*
	Glossostigma elatinoides
	Echinodorus tenellus
	Lilaeopsis novae-zelandiae
Animals	*Hemigrammus armstrongi*
	Crossocheilus siamensis
	Caridina japonica
	Otocinclus sp.

DATA

Date	September, 2006
Aquarium	W71 x D24 x H24 (in)
Lighting	NAG-150W Green (Solar I) x 3 units, turned on for 10 hours
Filter	Super Jet Filter ES-2400, Bio Rio
Substrate	Aqua Soil Amazonia, Power Sand Special L,
	Bacter 100, Clear Super, Tourmaline BC,
	Penac W for Aquarium, Penac P
CO₂	Pollen Glass Beetle 50,
	9 bubbles per second via CO₂ Beetle Counter
Aeration	14 hours after the light is turned off using Lily Pipe P-6

Additives	Brighty K; Green Brighty Special LIGHTS; Green Gain
Water Change	1/3 once a week
Water Quality	Temperature 79°F; pH 6.8; TH 50mg/l
Aquatic Plants	*Glossostigma elatinoides*
	Riccia fluitans
Animals	*Paracheirodon axelrodi*
	Caridina japonica

A New Material Creates a New Layout

Composition materials, such as rocks and driftwood, are indispensable for creating Nature Aquarium. The use of these materials defines the composition and renders a natural feel to a layout. An overall impression of a layout will look different when different types of layout materials are used, even if the layout is planted with the same plants and the same fish are placed in it. This is true with an Iwagumi layout as well. I used to use river rocks, such as Senmigawa-ishi and Hakkaiseki, in the early days.

ADA

With the introduction of petrified wood, Manten Stone, and Ryuo Stone that have different textures, images of created sceneries expanded from rivers to oceans and mountains. Even greater variations are possible by changing the types of aquatic plants that are combined with rocks in a layout.

Periodically I hear people complaining that they cannot create a good layout because they don't have shapely rocks or driftwood. I wonder if this is because they are trying to recreate an already existing layout with existing materials on hand. If this is the case,

it may be a good idea to go out themselves and look for rocks and driftwood in the outdoors. An idea of Nature Aquarium is something that is learned from nature in the first place. An idea about the outdoors is projected in an aquarium indoors. When you get tired of staring at an aquarium and layout materials, going out for fresh air can be quite refreshing. A change in the way a material is presented can change an impression greatly. While Ryuoseki can appear quite powerful and rugged if used in a somewhat upright position, it can create an easygoing and

expansive atmosphere if placed sideways, as in this aquascape. The concept of using rocks and driftwood in an aquarium did not exist in the past. Nowadays, the concept is accepted by many aquarists and is practiced in the world. It would be interesting to see an aquarist, undaunted and inquisitive, open up a new genre of aquarium culture with a new idea.

DATA

Date	/April, 2007
Aquarium	/W24 x D12 x H14 (in)
Lighting	/NA Lamp 36W Twin x 2 units (Solar II), turned on for 10 hours
Filter	/Super Jet Filter ES-600, Bio Rio, NA Carbon
Substrate	/Aqua Soil Amazonia, Bright Sand, Bacter 100, Clear Super, Penac W for Aquarium, Penac P
CO₂	/Pollen Glass, 3 bubbles per second via CO₂ Bubble Counter
Aeration	/14 hours after the light is turned off using Lily Pipe P-2
Additives	/Brighty K; Green Brighty STEP 2; ECA
Water Change	/1/3 once a week

Water Quality /Temperature 75°F; pH 6.8; TH 10mg/l

Aquatic Plants /*Rotala rotundifolia* (green)
Ludwigia arcuata
Myriophyllum mattogrossense (green)
Cryptocoryne wendtii (green)
Cryptocoryne petchii
Anubias barteri var. *nana* (narrow)
Microsorum sp.
Bolbitis heudelotii
Riccia fluitans
Fontinalis antipyretica

Animals /*Pseudomugil gertrudae*
Crossocheilus siamensis
Caridina japonica
Otocinclus sp.

DATA

Date /February, 2007
Aquarium /W24 x D12 x H14 (in)
Lighting /NA Lamp 36W Twin x 2 units (Solar II), turned on for 10 hours
Filter /Super Jet Filter ES-600, Bio Rio, NA Carbon
Substrate /Aqua Soil Amazonia, Bacter 100, Clear Super,
Penac W for Aquarium, Penac P
CO₂ /Pollen Glass, 3 bubbles per second via CO₂ Bubble Counter
Aeration /14 hours after the light is turned off using Lily Pipe P-2
Additives /Brighty K; Green Brighty STEP 2; ECA
Water Change /1/3 once a week
Water Quality /Temperature 75°F; pH 6.8; TH 10mg/l
Aquatic Plants /Wabi Kusa Stemmed Plants MIX
Glossostigma elatinoides
Eleocharis acicularis
Riccia fluitans
Fontinalis antipyretica
Animals /*Poecilia reticulata* var.
Caridina japonica
Otocinclus sp.

DATA

Date /May, 2005
Aquarium /W24 x D12 x H18 (in)
Lighting /NA Lamp 20W x 4 units, turned on for 10 hours
Filter /Super Jet Filter ES-600, Bio Rio
Substrate /Aqua Soil Amazonia, Power Sand Special S,
Bacter 100, Clear Super, Tourmaline BC,
Penac W for Aquarium, Penac P
CO₂ /Pollen Glass,
3 bubbles per second via CO₂ Bubble Counter
Aeration /14 hours after the light is turned off using
Lily Pipe P-2
Additives /Brighty K; Green Brighty STEP 2;
Green Brighty Special LIGHTS
Water Change /1/3 once a week
Water Quality /Temperature 79°F; pH 6.8; TH 20mg/l
Aquatic Plants /*Glossostigma elatinoides*
Echinodorus tenellus
Anubias barteri var. *nana* (narrow)

Microsorum sp.
Myriophyllum mattogrossense (green)
Rotala sp.
Rotala nanjean
Micranthemum unbrosum
Ludwigia arcuata
Rotala sp.
Eusteralis sp.
Rotala rotundifolia (green)
Riccia fluitans
Fontinalis antipyretica
Animals /*Inpaichthys kerri*
Hyphessobrycon herbertaxelrodi
Hyphessobrycon sp.
Hyphessobrycon amandae
Caridina japonica
Otocinclus sp.

DATA

Date	September, 2006
Aquarium	W71 x D24 x H24 (in)
Lighting	NAG-150W Green (Solar I) x 3 units, turned on for 10 hours
Filter	Super Jet Filter ES-2400, Bio Rio, NA Carbon
Substrate	Aqua Soil Amazonia, Power Sand L, Bacter 100, Clear Super, Tourmaline BC, Penac W for Aquarium, Penac P
CO₂	Pollen Glass Beetle 50, 6 bubbles per second via CO₂ Beetle Counter
Aeration	14 hours after the light is turned off using Lily Pipe P-6
Additives	Brighty K; Green Brighty STEP 2
Water Change	1/3 once a week
Water Quality	Temperature 77°F; pH 6.6; TH 20mg/l

Aquatic Plants	*Eleocharis vivipara*
	Echinodorus latifolius
	Echinodorus tenellus
	Glossostigma elatinoides
Animals	*Nematobrycon palmeri*
	Nematobrycon lacortei
	Crossocheilus siamensis
	Otocinclus sp.
	Caridina japonica

1: In the case of an Iwagumi layout, it is fine to lay the substrate somewhat thinner and more flat, since Aqua Soil is applied at the end through soil mounding work after arranging rocks. Rock selection and arrangement comes next. If the rocks are to be placed upright, Oyaishi, which is the largest rock, should be selected based on the guideline of its height being at least 2/3 of the height of an aquarium. The Oyaishi will appear well-balanced if it is placed toward either the left or right of the center of the aquarium using the Golden Ratio (1: 1.618) as a reference. In this layout, Oyaishi was placed somewhat left of the center by carefully examining its shape at the same time.

2: Next, the second rock was placed to the right of the Oyaishi. It was placed in the opposite direction to the orientation of the Oyaishi. The angles of the two rocks are extremely important. Therefore, once the rocks are placed, their angles and tilts must be examined from a viewpoint that is level with the rocks. Then, the positions of the rocks are finalized by making small adjustments to their angles. When arranging large rocks that become the primary part of an arrangement, arrangement work is always carried out by going through this scrutiny. Although the arranged rocks must be secured very well, the rocks will look more powerful if their angles appear somewhat unstable.

5: The line formed by rocks and the substrate is defined further by placing small Suteishi (sacrificing stones). The use of these rocks makes the rocks appear more naturally continuous. Although the placement of the large, primary rocks is important in Iwagumi, the appearance of the areas immediately around the rocks is also important for rendering a natural feel to a layout. The small rocks soften the strong impression of the large rocks that comprises the framework and create the sense of unity among the group of rocks. When the rock arrangement was finished, the soil was mounded using powder type Aqua Soil, and the ridges and surface line of the substrate were adjusted.

6: Planting started by placing small stones with *Riccia fluitans* secured with Riccia Line next to the arranged rocks. These rocks were placed side by side without leaving gaps as much as possible. While the use of larger stones would make this task faster and simpler, the careful placement of the smaller stones naturally creates a subtle undulation. *Hemianthus callitrichoides* "Cuba" and *Glossostigma elatinoides* were planted in front of the *Riccia* and next to the rocks using tweezers designed for aquatic plants. The powder type Aqua Soil that was placed over the substrate keeps the shallow rooted *H. callitrichoides* "Cuba" from lifting up.

3: Another rock was added on the left side of the Oyaishi in a similar orientation to the Oyaishi. However, one must be careful not to make its orientation parallel to that of the Oyaishi. Then, a relatively large rock was placed on the right side of the aquarium to keep the three rocks that were arranged in the left side in balance. This made the rock arrangement have a radially-oriented flow rather than having rocks in parallel to each other. It rendered a sense of upward thrust to each rock and created the dynamic impression of the overall Iwagumi. The direction and the overall picture of the Iwagumi started to emerge at this point.

4: Smaller rocks were added in between the four major rocks that comprised the framework as if to support the rocks. These Soeishi were placed carefully by making sure that their directions would not be parallel to each other. The four discrete rocks gained continuity on account of these small rocks.
Iwagumi is made with an odd number of rocks as a general rule. The addition of a small rock placed upright on the far right made the number of rocks playing the central role in the scenery to five. Because this small rock was placed toward the rear of the aquarium, it strengthened the sense of depth by visual effect compared to the large rock in the front.

7: After *Hemianthus callitrichoides* "Cuba", *Riccia fluitans*, and *Glossostigma elatinoides* were planted in the front of the aquarium, planting continued to the area around rocks. *Blyxa japonica* and *Echinodorus tenellus* that go well together in an Iwagumi layout were selected for the area. Planting *Blyxa* in between the five major rocks, which play the key role in the scenery of the overall Iwagumi layout, enables the rocks and aquatic plants to blend well. The natural feel of the layout will be enhanced as *Echinodorus* spreads runners between rocks and develops more leaves.

8: While short aquatic plants were planted along the baseline formed by Soeishi and Suteishi in the foreground of the Iwagumi, taller *Eleocharis vivipara* was planted in the background. *Eleocharis* has the effect of softening the overly strong impression of rocks. Background plants are often used to balance the strength and weakness of the impression of rocks at the end. Although *Eleocharis* requires some extra care, it is a useful plant for an Iwagumi since its tone (denseness) can be easily adjusted. The layout was completed by adding water at the end.

*The finished aquascape is shown in the next page.

DATA

Date	/July, 2005
Aquarium	/W71 x D24 x H24 (in)
Lighting	/NAG-150W Green (Solar I) x 3 units, turned on for 10 hours
Filter	/Super Jet Filter ES-2400, Bio Rio
Substrate	/Aqua Soil Amazonia, Power Sand Special L, Bacter 100, Clear Super, Penac W for Aquarium, Penac P
CO₂	/Pollen Glass Beetle 50, 6 bubbles per second via CO₂ Beetle Counter
Aeration	/14 hours after the light is turned off using Lily Pipe P-6
Additives	/Brighty K; Green Brighty STEP 2
Water Change	/1/3 once a week
Water Quality	/Temperature 77°F; pH 6.8; TH 30mg/l

Aquatic Plants	/*Hemianthus callitrichoides* "Cuba"
	Glossostigma elatinoides
	Echinodorus tenellus
	Eleocharis vivipara
	Blyxa japonica
	Riccia fluitans
Animals	/*Paracheirodon axelrodi*
	Caridina japonica
	Otocinclus sp.
	Crossocheilus siamensis

Japanese People's Attitude toward Living Things and the Environment

Honestly speaking, Japanese people's level of awareness toward the environment is less than second class. A lot of people may argue that to be otherwise. Japanese industries and economy that developed various technologies such as hybrid cars, TVs, and various other home appliances may be first class. However, our attitude toward the natural environment is absolutely disgraceful. We have very little appreciation of the idea that human beings and living creatures can coexist in a mutually beneficial way. On the other hand, one can easily tell that Europeans are serious about the environment and living creatures just by looking at their lifestyle.

In the case of Japan, people are complacent about the fact that

spraying agricultural chemicals is causing living creatures to disappear around us. This complacency is at the root of the problem. Although many Japanese do not even question about the way agrichemicals are used, herbicide use in Japan is quite extensive. A large amount of herbicide is used in the farmland around ADA headquarters, and not a single weed is visible on the footpath between rice paddies.

On the other hand, Germany and other advanced countries in Europe use very little pesticide chemicals and chemical fertilizers. Although the use of pesticide chemicals and chemical fertilizers is not banned, their contents must be listed on the product labels. Consumers are smart and very eager to find out the effect of a product on living creatures and the environment. In the countryside

of Europe, the long forgotten smell of farmyard manures permeates the area, rivers are clean, and grass is dense and green. Rivers with three-sided concrete revetments no longer exist. It was decided that it was not good to have rivers that could not support living things, and the concrete revetments were removed and rivers were returned to their original forms, spending a large amount of money since the 1970s. The effort paid off and the living creatures from the past are thriving and reproducing.

The release of the Japanese crested ibis to their natural habitat has made news in Japan, but I wonder if the released birds will settle in Sado Island. So much has changed in the very last environment where the Japanese crested ibis has been seen living. Rivers have been covered with three-sided concrete revetments, fields are

sprayed with pesticides, and power lines and billboards fill the skyline. I believe that restoring their environment should be the first priority. It makes no sense to return the birds to Sado Island without first stopping the pesticide spray, eliminating power lines, and getting motivated to fundamentally improve the environment. What good does it do to keep the birds by flying in their food, the Oriental weather loach fish, from the surrounding prefectures? It is great if the Japanese crested ibis can become the symbol of environmental improvement. However, raising them without improving the environment makes no sense. It seems preposterous to restore Japanese crested ibis to the environment while ignoring the fact that a vast number of living things are facing extinction.

DATA

Date	July, 2007
Aquarium	W47 x D18 x H24 (in)
Lighting	NAG-150W Green (Solar I) x 2 units, turned on for 10 hours
Filter	Super Jet Filter ES-1200, Bio Rio
Substrate	Aqua Soil Amazonia II, Power Sand Special L, Bacter 100, Clear Super, Tourmaline BC, Penac W for Aquarium, Penac P
CO₂	Pollen Glass Beetle 50, 5 bubbles per second via CO₂ Beetle Counter
Aeration	14 hours after the light is turned off using Lily Pipe P-4
Additives	Brighty K; Green Brighty STEP 2
Water Change	1/3 once a week

Water Quality	Temperature 79°F; pH 7.0; TH 100mg/l
Aquatic Plants	*Riccia fluitans*
	Glossostigma elatinoides
	Echinodorus tenellus
	Eleocharis acicularis
	Eleocharis vivipara
Animals	*Hemigrammus armstrongi*
	Caridina japonica
	Otocinclus **sp.**

DATA

Date	October, 2007
Aquarium	W35 x D18 x H24 (in)
Lighting	NAG-150W Green (Solar I) x 1.5 units, turned on for 10 hours
Filter	Super Jet Filter ES-1200, Bio Rio, NA Carbon
Substrate	Aqua Soil Amazonia II, Power Sand Special L, Bacter 100,
	Clear Super, Penac W for Aquarium, Penac P, Tourmaline BC
CO₂	Pollen Glass Large 30, 4 bubbles per second via CO₂ Beetle Counter
Aeration	14 hours after the light is turned off using Lily Pipe P-4
Additives	Brighty K; Green Brighty STEP 2
Water Change	1/3 once a week
Water Quality	Temperature 81°F; pH 7.4; TH 100mg/l

Aquatic Plants	*Riccia fluitans*
	Glossostigma elatinoides
	Echinodorus tenellus
Animals	*Sawbwa resplens*
	Caridina japonica
	Otocinclus sp.

DATA
Date   /March, 2006
Aquarium   /W24 x D12 x H14 (in)
Lighting   /NA Lamp 36W Twin x 2 units (Solar II),
               turned on for 10 hours
Filter   /Super Jet Filter ES-600, Anthracite, Bio Rio
Substrate   /Aqua Soil Amazonia, Power Sand Special S, Bacter 100,
               Clear Super, Tourmaline BC, Penac W for Aquarium,
               Penac P
CO₂   /Pollen Glass TYPE-2, 3 bubbles per second via CO₂
               Bubble Counter
Aeration   /14 hours after the light is turned off using Lily Pipe P-2
Additives   /Brighty K; Green Brighty STEP 2
Water Change /1/3 once a week
Water Quality /Temperature 77°F; pH 6.8; TH 30mg/l
Aquatic Plants/*Glossostigma elatinoides*
               Echinodorus tenellus
               Blyxa japonica
               Eleocharis vivipara
               Riccia fluitans
Animals   /*Inpaichthys kerri*
               Caridina japonica
               Otocinclus sp.

DATA
Date   /March, 2006
Aquarium   /W24 x D12 x H14 (in)
Lighting   /NA Lamp 36W Twin x 2 units (Solar II),
               turned on for 10 hours
Filter   /Super Jet Filter ES-600, NA Carbon, Bio Rio
Substrate   /Aqua Soil Amazonia, Rio Negro Sand,
               Power Sand Special S, Bacter 100, Clear Super,
               Tourmaline BC, Penac W for Aquarium, Penac P
CO₂   /Pollen Glass TYPE-2, 3 bubbles per second via CO₂
               Bubble Counter
Aeration   /14 hours after the light is turned off using Lily Pipe P-2
Additives   /Brighty K; Green Brighty STEP 2; ECA; Green Gain
Water Change /1/3 once a week
Water Quality /Temperature 77°F; pH 6.8; TH 20mg/l
Aquatic Plants/*Micranthemum unbrosum*
               Rotala nanjean
               Rotara rotundifolia (green)
               Rotala rotundifolia
               Myriophyllum mattogrossense (green)
               Microsorum sp.
               Bolbitis heudelotii
               Riccia fluitans
               Fontinalis antipyretica
Animals   /*Pseudomugil gertrudae*
               Crossocheilus siamensis
               Caridina japonica
               Otocinclus sp.

DATA

Date / September, 2006
Aquarium / W47 x D18 x H24 (in)
Lighting / NAG-150W Green (Solar I) x 2 units, turned on for 10 hours
Filter / Super Jet Filter ES-1200, Bio Rio, NA Carbon
Substrate / Aqua Soil Amazonia, Power Sand Special L, Bacter 100, Clear Super,
Tourmaline BC, Penac W for Aquarium, Penac P
CO₂ / Pollen Glass Beetle 40, 4 bubbles per second via CO₂ Beetle Counter
Aeration / 14 hours after the light is turned off using Lily Pipe P-4
Additives / Brighty K; Green Brighty STEP 2
Water Change / 1/3 once a week
Water Quality / Temperature 77°F; pH 6.8; TH 50mg/l
Aquatic Plants / *Eleocharis vivipara*
Blyxa japonica

Lilaeopsis novae-zelandiae
Hemianthus callitrichoides "Cuba"
Animals / *Hyphessobrycon sweglesi*
Crossocheilus siamensis
Caridina japonica
Otocinclus sp.

DATA

Date	October, 2008
Aquarium	W71 x D24 x H24 (in)
Lighting	NAG-150W Green (Solar I) x 3 units, turned on for 10 hours
Filter	Super Jet Filter ES-2400, Bio Rio L, NA Carbon
Substrate	Aqua Soil Amazonia, Power Sand Special L,
	Bacter 100, Clear Super, Tourmaline BC,
	Penac W for Aquarium, Penac P
CO_2	Pollen Glass Beetle 50, 6 bubbles per second via CO_2
	Beetle Counter
Aeration	14 hours after the light is turned off using Lily Pipe P-6
Additives	Brighty K; Green Brighty STEP 2
Water Change	1/3 once a week
Water Quality	Temperature 77°F; pH 6.8; TH 20mg/l

Aquatic Plants	*Eleocharis vivipara*
	Eleocharis acicularis
Animals	*Paracheirodon simulans*
	Crossocheilus siamensis
	Caridina japonica
	Otocinclus sp.

Zen Aquarium

A spacious Iwagumi layout with one type of fish and simple plant-ing is very popular overseas, as well as in Japan. Nature Aquarium layouts that I create are called Zen Aquarium in Italy and other European countries. Since the Zen part of the name seems to relate to Zen Buddhism, I suspect that the strong impression of an Iwagumi layout might have been the reason for the coined name. Some people might have associated the way that rocks are arranged in a layout with the dry, garden style of Japanese gardens called Karesansui in Zen temples, and also Kare-sansui with Zen Buddhism. Since Zen Buddhism is well known among

DATA
Date   October, 2008
Aquarium   W71 x D24 x H24 (in)
Lighting   NAG-150W Green (Solar I) x 3 units, turned on for 10 hours
Filter   Super Jet Filter ES-2400, Bio Rio, NA Carbon
Substrate   Aqua Soil Amazonia, Power Sand Special L,
            Bacter 100, Clear Super, Tourmaline BC,
            Penac W for Aquarium, Penac P
CO₂   Pollen Glass Beetle 50, 6 bubbles per second via CO₂

Water Change   1/3 once a week
Water Quality   Temperature 77°F; pH 6.8; TH 20mg/l
Aquatic Plants   *Glossostigma elatinoides*
                 Riccia fluitans
                 Echinodorus tenellus
                 Eleocharis vivipara
Animals   *Puntius denisonii*
                 Caridina japonica

Farmer's Claims and My Contention

I have been quite annoyed by the gap between the environment found in an aquarium with vigorously growing aquatic plants and the reality of the eroding, natural environment. I cannot stand looking at dead grass and trees. I love dense, energetically growing trees and grass that are full of life. It's natural that grass dies down in autumn, but I cannot tolerate grass being killed artificially by an

cide around ADA's premises. Farmers spray herbicides on fields and on every footpath between rice paddies because of the fear of attracting insect pests. They routinely spray on a daily basis. They say that others will suffer if one stops spraying. Not a single farmer laments that living creatures will disappear if they keep on spraying herbicides. I understand their difficult situation, but if this problem is left alone, the land will eventually be so contaminated that nothing can live on it. Sadly, this is a reality, but I want people to stop and think. Do you think the rice that is grown in a field where

no organism can live will still be tasty? I don't think I want to put that in my mouth.

Aside from this, children used to make garlands with white clover and would give it to someone they liked. Nowadays white clover has been eradicated with herbicides. Tree frogs that used to be all around us have drastically decreased in number, and it is becoming difficult to find an overwintered, adult tree frog. I don't know if herbicide is the cause of this, but it is clear that something unusual is happening in the environment around us. The environ-

ment would restore itself normally if we left it alone. The area around ADA's premises used to be a lagoon. Seeds of various aquatic plants can be unearthed if we dig around. Unlike terrestrial plants, aquatic plants have seed capsules that allow their seeds to remain dormant in the ground until all germination conditions are met. Therefore, in the case of aquatic plants, there still is a hope to recover these seeds and bring them back. However, it is very difficult to bring back the living creatures that have disappeared.

DATA

Date / October, 2009

Aquarium / W71 x D24 x H24 (cm)

Lighting / NAG-150W Green (Solar I) x 3 units, turned on for 10 hours

Filter / Super Jet Filter ES-2400, Bio Rio L, NA Carbon

Substrate / Aqua Soil Amazonia II, Power Sand Special L,
Bacter 100, Clear Super, Tourmaline BC,
Penac W for Aquarium, Penac P

CO₂ / Pollen Glass Beetle 50 x 2 units, 5 bubbles per second
via CO₂ Beetle Counter x 2 units

Aeration / 14 hours after the light is turned off using Lily Pipe P-6

Additives / Brighty K; Green Brighty STEP 2; ECA

Water Change / 1/3 once a week

Water Quality / Temperature 77°F; pH 6.6; TH 20mg/l

Aquatic Plants / *Hemianthus callitrichoides* "Cuba"

Animals / *Paracheirodon axelrodi*
Crossocheilus siamensis
Caridina japonica
Otocinclus sp.

DATA

Date	November, 2008
Aquarium	W47 x D18 x H24 (in)
Lighting	NAG-150W Green (Solar I) x 2 units, turned on for 10 hours
Filter	Super Jet Filter ES-1200, Bio Rio, NA Carbon
Substrate	Aqua Soil Amazonia, Forest Sand Branco,
	Power Sand Special L, Bacter 100, Clear Super,
	Tourmaline BC, Penac W for Aquarium, Penac P
CO₂	Pollen Glass Beetle 40, 5 bubbles per second via CO₂
	Beetle Counter
Aeration	14 hours after the light is turned off using Lily Pipe P-4
Additives	Brighty K; Green Brighty STEP 2
Water Change	1/3 once a week

Water Quality	Temperature 77°F; pH 6.8; TH 20mg/l
Aquatic Plants	*Rotala rotundifolia*
	Rotala nanjean
	Rotala sp.
	Rotala macrandra sp.
	Rotala rotundifolia (green)
	Ludwigia arcuata
	Myriophyllum matogrossense (green)
	Pogostemon sp "Dassen"
	Nesaea pedicellata
	Lilaeopsis novae-zelandiae
	Fontinalis antipyretica

	Cryptocoryne petchii
	Cryptocoryne wendtii var. "real green"
	Anubias barteri var. *nana* "yellow heart"
	Microsorum sp.
	Bolbitis heudelotii
Animals	*Hyphessobrycon rosaceus* var.
	Hyphessobrycon megalopterus
	Hyphessobrycon sweglesi
	Crossocheilus siamensis
	Caridina japonica
	Otocinclus sp.

DATA

Date	September, 2009
Aquarium	W47 x D18 x H24 (in)
Lighting	NAG-150W Green (Solar I) x 2 units, turned on for 10 hours
Filter	Super Jet Filter ES-1200, Bio Rio
Substrate	Aqua Soil Amazonia, Power Sand Special L, Bacter 100, Clear Super, Tourmaline BC, Penac W for Aquarium, Penac P
CO_2	Pollen Glass Beetle 50, 4 bubbles per second via CO_2 Beetle Counter
Aeration	14 hours after the light is turned off using Lily Pipe P-4
Additives	Brighty K; Green Brighty STEP 2; Green Gain
Water Change	1/3 once a week
Water Quality	Temperature 75°F; pH 7.0; TH 100mg/l
Aquatic Plants	*Riccia fluitans*
	Hemianthus callitrichoides "Cuba"
	Eleocharis acicularis
Animals	*Inpaichthys kerri*
	Crossocheilus siamensis
	Caridina japonica
	Otocinclus sp.

DATA

Date   October, 2009

Aquarium   W35 x D18 x H18 (in)

Lighting   NAG-150W Green/NA Lamp 36W Twin x 2 units
            (Grand Solar I), turned on for 10 hours

Filter   Super Jet Filter ES-600, Bio Rio

Substrate   Aqua Soil Amazonia II, Power Sand Special M,
            Bacter 100, Clear Super, Tourmaline BC,
            Penac W for Aquarium, Penac P

CO_2 Pollen Glass Large 30, 4 bubbles per second via CO_2

DATA

Date	/October, 2009	Water Quality /Temperature 77°F; pH 6.6; TH 10mg/l	*Fontinalis antipyretica*	*Hyphessobrycon sweglesi*
Aquarium	/W94.5 x D24 x H24 (in)	Aquatic Plants /*Hygrophila polysperma*	*Bolbitis heudelotii*	*Hemigrammus erythrozonus*
Lighting	/NAG-150W Green/NA Lamp 36W Twin x 2 units	*Hygrophila stricta*	*Microsorum* sp.	*Mikrogeophagus ramirezi*
	(Grand Solar I) x 4 units	*Rotala indica*	*Eleochalis acicularis*	*Inpaichthys kerri*
Filter	/Super Jet Filter ES-2400 x 2 units, Bio Rio	*Pogostemon* sp. "Dassen"	*Echinodorus latifolius*	*Hemigrammus armstrongi*
Substrate	/Aqua Soil Amazonia, Power Sand Special L, Bacter 100,	*Alternanthera reineckii* "Lilacina"	*Glossostigma elatinoides*	*Hyphessobrycon herbertaxelrodi*
	Clear Super, Tourmaline BC, Penac W for Aquarium, Penac P	*Myriophyllum matogrossense*	*Anubias barteri* var. *nana*	*Aphyocharax rathbuni*
CO₂	/Pollen Glass Beetle 50, 8 bubbles per second via CO₂	*Ludwigia arcuata*	*Anubias barteri* var. *nana* "yellow herat"	*Hyphessobrycon rosaceus* var.
	Beetle Counter	*Ammannia latifolia*	*Cryptocoryne wendtii* (Mi Oya)	*Hemigrammus pulcher*
Aeration	/14 hours after the light is turned off using Pollen Glass Beetle	*Ammannia gracilis*	*Cryptocoryne petchii*	*Colisa sota* var.
	50 for AIR	*Rotala rotundifolia* (green)	*Cryptocoryne wendtii* (green)	*Caridina japonica*
Additives	/Brighty K; Green Brighty STEP 2; ECA; Green Gain	*Rotala rotundifolia*	Animals/*Trigonostigma heteromorpha*	*Otocinclus* sp.
Water Change	/1/4 once a week	*Blyxa novoguineensis*	*Paracheirodon axelrodi*	

Creating Light and Dark Areas in a Layout

In Nature Aquarium, a natural feel is created by using characteristically different sciophytic and heliophytic plants. Since the colors of these aquatic plants also tend to be either in dark and light or deep and pale contrast, they help to create a change in a layout. The light and dark contrast can also be expressed in a layout with the use of composition materials, such as rocks and driftwood, instead of aquatic plants. If a rock is tilted forward, it creates a dark area in a layout, but if it is tilted toward the back, it does not. In the case of driftwood, while it casts a shade underneath, if the driftwood is tilted forward, the size of the shaded area increases. As the size of the shaded area increases, it strengthens the dark impression. As it decreases, it strengthens the light impression. The impression of an overall layout can be changed effortlessly by combining this technique and the use of sciophytic plants and heliophytic plants.

DATA

Date	December, 2008
Aquarium	W35 x D18 x H18 (in)
Lighting	NAG-150W Green (Solar I) x 1.5 units, turned on for 10 hours
Filter	Super Jet Filter ES-1200, Bio Rio M, NA Carbon
Substrate	Aqua Soil Amazonia, Bright Sand, Power Sand Special L,
	Bacter 100, Clear Super, Penac W for Aquarium,
	Penac P, Tourmaline BC
CO_2	Pollen Glass Large 30, 3 bubbles per second via CO_2

Water Quality	Temperature 77°F; pH 6.8; TH 20mg/l
Aquatic Plants	*Alternanthera reineckii*
	Ludwigia arcuata
	Rotala rotundifolia
	Microsorum sp.
	Marsilea crenata
	Lilaeopsis novae-zelandiae
	Fontinalis antipyretica

DATA

Date	October, 2009
Aquarium	W35 x D18 x H24 (in)
Lighting	NAG-150W Green (Solar I), turned on for 10 hours
Filter	Super Jet Filter ES-1200, Bio Rio
Substrate	Aqua Soil Amazonia II, Power Sand Special M, Bacter 100, Clear Super, Penac W for Aquarium, Penac P, Tourmaline BC
CO₂	Pollen Glass Large 30, 4 bubbles per second via CO₂ Bubble Counter
Aeration	14 hours after the light is turned off using Lily Pipe P-4
Additives	Brighty K; Green Brighty STEP 2; Green Gain
Water Change	1/3 once a week
Water Quality	Temperature 77°F; pH 6.8; TH 10mg/l
Aquatic Plants	*Eleocharis vivipara*
	Echinodorus angstifolia
	Vallisneria nana
	Fontinalis antipyretica
	Blyxa aubertii
	Lilaeopsis novae-zelandiae

Cryptocoryne petchii

Cryptocoryne wendtii (green)

Cryptocoryne willisii

Cryptocoryne lucens

Cryptocoryne undulata (red)

Animals *Puntius titteya*

Crossocheilus siamensis

Caridina japonica

Otocinclus sp.

DATA

Date	/October, 2009
Aquarium	/W24 x D12 x H7 (in)
Lighting	/NA Lamp 36W Twin x 2 units (Solar II), turned on for 10 hours
Filter	/External Filter, Bio Rio L, NA Carbon
Substrate	/Aqua Soil Amazonia II, Power Sand Special L, Bacter 100, Clear Super, Penac W for Aquarium, Penac P, Tourmaline BC
CO₂	/Pollen Glass Mini, 2 bubbles per second via CO₂ Bubble Counter
Additives	/Brighty K; Green Brighty STEP 2
Water Change	/1/3 once a week
Water Quality	/Temperature 77°F; pH 6.6; TH 20mg/l

Aquatic Plants	/*Riccia fluitans*
	Hemianthus callitrichoides "Cuba"
Animals	/*Boraras brigittae*
	Crossocheilus siamensis
	Caridina japonica

The Sense of Scale for an Aquascape

Looking at this aquascape, what size do you think this aquarium is? Although it may look like a large aquarium with a panoramic view, it is a shallow 24 x 12 x 7 inches aquarium with only an 8-gallon capacity. I placed a rock into the aquarium that I bought when I traveled to China and planted *Hemianthus callitricoides* and *Riccia* around it. I also used small fish, *Boraras brigittae*, so as not to spoil the sense of scale. While it is normal to make a large aquarium appear large, the fun is in making a small aquarium look really big. Since this aquarium is shallow and lit with a pendant type Solar II fixture, it is easy to do maintenance in it. Although the aquatic plants grow fast, this aquarium is just the right size for spending time and effort to maintain an aquascape.

DATA
Date /September, 2009
Aquarium /W138 x D29.5 x H29.5 (in)
Lighting /NAG-150W Green/NA Lamp 36W Twin x 2 units
         (Grand Solar I) x 6 units, turned on for 10 hours
Filter /External filter, Bio Rio L, NA Carbon
Substrate /Aqua Soil Amazonia II, Power Sand Special L, Bacter 100,
         Clear Super, Tourmaline BC, Penac W for Aquarium,
         Penac P
CO₂ /Pollen Glass Beetle 50 x 4 units, 5 bubbles per second via
     CO₂ Beetle Counter x 4 units
Aeration /Turned on after lights are turned off with NA Control Timer
Additives /Brighty K; Green Brighty STEP 2; ECA
Water Change /1/3 once a week
Water Quality /Temperature 77°F; pH 6.6; TH 20mg/l

Aquatic Plants /*Aponogeton rigidifolius*
                Aponogeton madagascariensis
                Crinum calamistratum
                Vallisneria nana
                Eleocharis vivipara
                Echinodorus angstifolia
                Echinodorus tenellus
                Glossostigma elatinoides
                Riccia fluitans

Animals /*Hyphessobrycon sweglesi*
         Paracheirodon axelrodi
         Hemigrammus bleheri
         Hyphessobrycon herbertaxelrodi
         Hemigrammus armstrongi
         Inpaichthys kerri
         Crossocheilus siamensis
         Caridina japonica

Changed Environment

How many people are aware that the environment has changed this much in the past 40 to 50 years? Japan placed a lot of priority on the productivity of our industries and began transforming the land in the early 1960s. Dump trucks ran around all the time, even in the countryside of Niigata where I live, and the Yoroigata where I played in my childhood was also reclaimed. So-called land improvement work took place throughout the nation and people were looking at that as a symbol of modernization. A huge amount of agrichemicals were sprayed on rice paddies and their footpaths, and the rivers were fitted with straight, three-sided concrete revetments. The splendid nature that existed in mid 1950s disappeared in a blink of an eye, but no one talked about it at the time.

However, it was obvious to me for I was diving in a lagoon and rivers to catch fish. Concrete clad rivers not only changed their appearances but also lost their abilities to support living things. I was instinctively terrified to see the water filled with agrichemicals and run in a straight line. I had very mixed emotions looking at the transformed appearance of nature. Come to think of it, back then I was swimming in a nearby river and kingfishers were still around us. Flying insects hatched out on the water surface in the evening and fishes jumped out of the water to eat them. The river is now a river of death. When it comes to soil, there is living soil and dead soil. Various microorganisms exist in the living soil and keep the soil clean. The microorganisms play an important role in the growth of plants. Human beings are predicted to become extinct in five years if microorganisms disappeared from the Earth. The rice paddies around me had lost microorganisms due to agrichemicals, and oil is floating on their surfaces. In fact, the soil is dead. No living organism is found in such a place. It is hard to find even a mystery snail.

If we still had lagoons and rivers filled with various ecosystems of the old days, I think that we would not have the global warming issue. CO_2 emission is often discussed as the cause of the global warming. However, it is important not only to discuss the issue but also to restore the ecosystems and figure out correctly how many living organisms are around us. Although CO_2 is a real problem, it seems scarier to me that no one recognized the fact that the environment around us has been destroyed so much. Therefore, I have been devoting myself to the world of aquarium called Nature Aquarium as if to search for an ideal environment. Now I want to engage in raising people's consciousness toward the environment through Nature Aquarium.

DATA

Date	October, 2009
Aquarium	W35 x D18 x H18 (in)
Lighting	NAG-150W Green/NA Lamp 36W Twin x 2 units
	(Grand Solar I), turned on for 10 hours
Filter	Super Jet Filter ES-600, Bio Rio
Substrate	Aqua Soil Amazonia II, Power Sand Special M,
	Bacter 100, Clear Super, Tourmaline BC,
	Penac W for Aquarium, Penac P

CO₂	Pollen Glass Large 30, 4 bubbles per second via CO₂
	Beetle Counter
Aeration	14 hours after the light is turned off using Lily Pipe P-4
Additives	Brighty K; Green Brighty STEP 2; Green Gain
Water Change	1/3 once a week
Water Quality	Temperature 77°F; pH 7.0; TH 20mg/l
Aquatic Plants	*Eleocharis vivipara*
	Echinodorus tenellus
	Glossostigma elatinoides
	Eleocharis acicularis
	Lilaeopsis novae-zelandiae
Animals	*Nematobrycon lacortei*
	Caridina japonica
	Otocinclus sp.

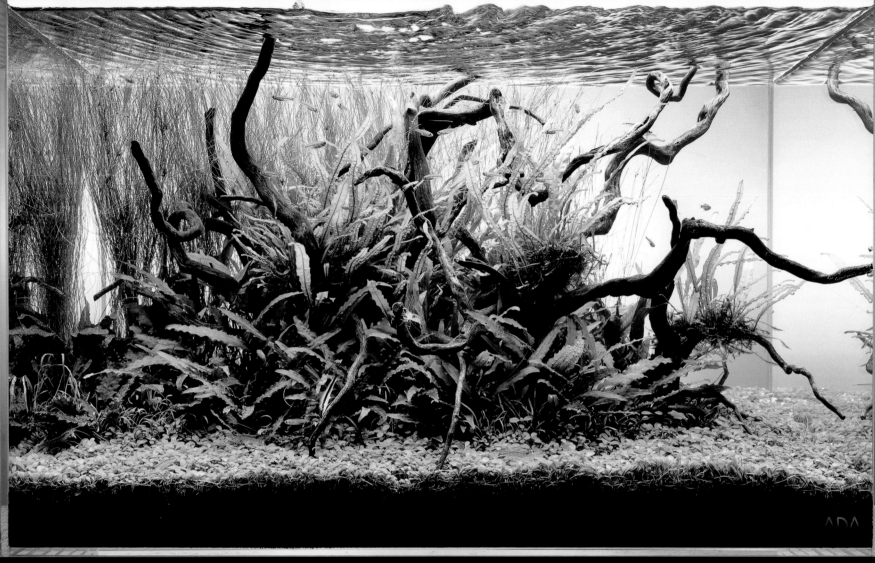

DATA

Date	October, 2009
Aquarium	W24 x D12 x H14 (in)
Lighting	NA Lamp 36W Twin x 2 units (Solar II), turned on for 10 hours
Filter	Super Jet Filter ES-600, Bio Rio
Substrate	Aqua Soil Amazonia II, Power Sand Special S, Bacter 100, Clear Super, Penac W for Aquarium, Penac P, Tourmaline BC
CO_2	Pollen Glass, 3 bubbles per second via CO_2 Bubble Counter
Aeration	14 hours after the light is turned off using Lily Pipe P-2
Additives	Brighty K; Green Brighty STEP 2; Green Gain
Water Change	1/3 once a week
Water Quality	Temperature 77°F; pH 6.8; TH 20mg/l
Aquatic Plants	*Eleocharis vivipara*
	Microsorum sp.

Cryptocoryne wendtii (**Tropica**)

Cryptocoryne petchii

Animals *Microrasbora kubotai*

Crossocheilus siamensis

Caridina japonica

Otocinclus sp.

Full-Scale Water Area

Because of the size limitations of an aquarium, a layout in an aquarium tends to look like a small replica of nature. This depends on the scale of the image of natural scenery that one tries to create in a layout. In the case of an Iwagumi layout, created in a small aquarium in the image of vast grassland, naturally the scale ratio becomes large. On the other hand, an aquascape in the image of underwater scenery can be created practically in full scale in a large aquarium. Since the aquarium on this page has a good depth with dimensions of 71 x 47 inches, it was possible to use large driftwood pieces. It has overflow boxes in the rear left and right corners. This requires U-shaped composition, with driftwood arranged inevitably in the left and right sides of the aquarium to hide the overflow boxes. This composition actually accentuates the depth perception of the aquascape. Willow moss is growing on the surfaces of driftwood pieces in a natural fashion, enhancing the natural feel of the aquascape. The spacious underwater scenery makes viewers feel as if they are diving underwater.

This aquascape was created in an open top aquarium with driftwood protruding above the water surface. While maintaining the aquascape for a long time, *Bolbitis heudelotti* that was growing right beneath the water surface gradually developed leaves above the water surface. I am often asked how to get *Bolbitis* to develop emersed-grown leaves like this. This did not happen in a half or one year period. It gradually got to this state over a three to four year period. This type of aquascape is only possible in an open top aquarium maintained for a long period of time.

Six Grand Solar I fixtures, which can turn on metal halide lamps and power compacts lamps simultaneously, were installed to realize an open top layout in this large unusual aquarium. The intense light similar to sunlight enables *Bolbitis* to grow emersed-grown leaves suitable for the environment. One can say that this is a life-size aquascape that has brought out the natural ability of an aquatic plant.

DATA
Date	August, 2009
Aquarium	W71 x D47 x H24 (in)
Lighting	NAG-150W Green/NA Lamp 36W Twin x 2 units (Grand Solar I) x 6 units, turned on for 10 hours
Filter	Original Overflow filtration system
Substrate	Aqua Soil Amazonia, Rio Negro Sand, Power Sand Special L, Bacter 100, Clear Super, Tourmaline BC, Penac W for Aquarium, Penac P
CO_2	Direct injection in the inflow pipe coming from the pump head inside the filter sump, 6 bubbles per second via CO_2 Beetle Counter x 2 units
Additives	Brighty K; Green Brighty STEP 2; ECA
Water Change	1/3 once a week
Water Quality	Temperature 81°F; pH 7.0; TH 20mg/l
Aquatic Plants	*Microsorum* sp.
	Bolbitis heudelotii
	Fontinalis antipyretica
	Cryptocoryne retrospiralis
	Cryptocoryne wendtii (green)
	Cryptocoryne petchii
Animals	*Puntius denisonii*
	Puntius sp.
	Rasbora bankanensis
	Puntius rhomboocellatus
	Rasbora trilineata
	Rasbora einthovenii
	Caridina japonica
	Otocinclus sp.

DATA

Date — October, 2008
Aquarium — W71 x D24 x H24 (in)
Lighting — NAG-150W Green (Solar I) x 3 units, turned on for 10 hours
Filter — Super Jet Filter ES-2400, Bio Rio, NA Carbon
Substrate — Aqua Soil Amazonia II, Power Sand L, Bacter 100,
  Clear Super, Tourmaline BC, Penac W for Aquarium, Penac P
CO₂ — Pollen Glass Beetle 50, 6 bubbles per second via CO₂ Beetle
  Counter
Aeration — 14 hours after the light is turned off using Lily Pipe P-6
Additives — Brighty K; Green Brighty STEP 2

Water Change — 1/3 once a week
Water Quality — Temperature 77°F; pH 6.6; TH 20mg/l
Aquatic Plants — *Cryptocoryne retrospiralis*
  Echinodorus tenellus
  Lilaeopsis novae zelandiae
  Glossostigma elatinoides
Animals — *Nematobrycon palmeri*
  Crossocheilus siamensis
  Otocinclus sp.
  Caridina japonica

Nature Aquarium Gaining Popularity in the World

Nature Aquarium World Book 1, published in 1992, was translated into various languages and led to the increase in popularity of Nature Aquarium overseas. As its natural layout style became widely recognized, I started getting requests for lectures and layout demonstrations from all over the world. Although I try to comply with as many requests as possible as my schedule permits, there is a limit as to how many I can handle. Rather than trying to do it all by myself, I felt it necessary to increase the popularity of an aquatic plant layout and to develop leaders who can carry out the job successfully in the world. I did so by teaching the

philosophy of Nature Aquarium that I have been advocating for many years and how to apply its concepts and systems correctly. Luckily, there are many young people in the world who are serious about learning Nature Aquarium. Therefore, I give seminars that are a few days long for these people in the Gallery. These seminars cover a broad range of topics, such as the basic method of creating Nature Aquarium, its maintenance method, and aquatic plant rearrangement called Sozo Haishoku. Seminar participants also arrange rocks, and I critique and make corrections to their arrangements.

In one of the seminars, there was a session in which I created an

Iwagumi layout with rocks that participants had selected. Approximately twenty participants selected rocks out of a mountain of rocks, all with very serious expressions on their faces. They evaluated each other's selections and voted for the best rock. Naturally some rocks got a lot of votes and some not so many. Looking at this result, I declared that I would use the least popular rocks that did not get any vote. Although all the participants looked quite surprised at this, I wanted them to learn that a layout can be created with any rock by making the most of the rock's character. The least popular rocks were a pair of rocks chosen by a Polish participant. He said that the rocks were a pair, like a man and

wife, and wanted me to use them together. So I placed the two rocks with the same characteristics in a layout in a manner that would create a natural flow, and I created a clearly defined space between the two to avoid a heavy impression. Planting was done so that the space in the center was not filled. The finished aquascape had unique perspectives. Iwagumi layouts are quite popular overseas as well as in Japan, and the participants must have been looking forward to the finished aquascape. I hope that the participants of those seminars will go back to their own countries with their acquired knowledge and contribute to increasing the popularity of Nature Aquarium even more.

DATA

Date / October, 2009

Aquarium / W71 x D24 x H24 (in)

Lighting / NAG-150W Green/NA Lamp 36W Twin x 2 units
(Grand Solar I) x 3 units, turned on for 10 hours

Filter / Super Jet Filter ES-2400, Bio Rio L, NA Carbon

Substrate / Aqua Soil Amazonia II, Power Sand Special L,
Bacter 100, Clear Super, Tourmaline BC,
Penac W for Aquarium, Penac P

CO₂ / Pollen Glass Beetle 50 x 2 units, 5 bubbles per
second via CO₂ Beetle Counter x 2 units

Aeration / 14 hours after the light is turned off using Pollen Glass
Beetle 50 for AIR with NA Control Timer

Additives / Brighty K; Green Brighty STEP 2; ECA

Water Change / 1/3 once a week

Water Quality / Temperature 77°F; pH 6.6; TH 20mg/l

Aquatic Plants / *Hemianthus callitrichoides* "Cuba"

Cryptocoryne wendtii (green)

Cryptocoryne wendtii (brown)

Cryptocoryne albida

Cryptocoryne petchii

Lilaeopsis novae zelandiae

Echinodorus tenellus

Eleocharis acicularis

Anubias barteri var. *nana* "petit"

Blyxa japonica

Vallisneria nana

Rotala rotundifolia

Ludwigia arcuata

Ludwigia ovaris

Pogostemon sp. "Dassen"

Microsorum sp.

Animals / *Rasboroides vaterifloris*

Crossocheilus siamensis

Otocinclus sp.

Caridina japonica

A Natural Feel Created by Aquatic Plants

When you look at a dense, old-growth forest or a grassy field, do you find it untidy? Or do you find it orderly? When asked such a question, I suspect that the majority of people would say that they find it untidy looking. However, while plants in nature appear untidy at a glance, plants mingle well with each other and grow densely in a logical manner in a sense. In an old-growth forest, while various types of trees compete, there exists an undergrowth of sciophytic plants that grow in shades and there are vines that twist around tree trunks and branches. Incorporating such a natural appearance into a layout is an important concept for expressing natural feel in Nature Aquarium. In this layout, in addition to the various stem plants and *Cryptocoryne*, *Eleocharis aciluralis*, *Lilaeopsis novae-zelandiae*, and *Hemianthus callitrichoides* "Cuba" blend well as undergrowth. Although heliophytic stem plants and sciophytic Cryptocoryne have different growing conditions, stem plants occupy the bright environment in the upper layer, and *Cryptocoryne* spreads its leaves wide in the shade of stem plants and driftwood. The undergrowth grows around the base of the *Cryptocoryne*, filling every space that is suitable for its growth without a gap. If plants are planted in appropriate locations by considering the biological characteristics of individual aquatic plants during planning, natural looking bushes of aquatic plants develop by simply allowing them to grow on their own.

The latest image of the 13-foot tank at Amano's private residence. There is almost no algae growing and water is crystal-clear. Composition of water plants and fishes has changed slightly over time due to their growth and life span.
(Photograph: October, 2009)

DATA

Date	/October, 2009	Aquatic Plants	/*Microsorum* sp.	*Hemigrammus bleheri*
Aquarium	/W157.5 x D59 x H59 (in)		*Bolbitis heudelotii*	*Hemigrammus ocellifer*
Lighting	/NAG-150W Green x 16 units, NA Lamp 40W x 9 units		*Crinum calamistratum*	*Arnoldichthys spilopterus*
Filter	/Original Overflow filtration system		*Cryptocoryne crispatula* var. *balansae*	*Sphaerichthys osphromenoides*
Substrate	/Aqua Soil Amazonia, Forest Sand Branco,		*Ceratopteris cornuta*	*Betta strohi*
	Power Sand Special L, Bacter 100, Clear Super,		*Anubias barteri* var. *nana*	*Betta* sp. *Mahachai*
	Tourmaline BC, Penac W for Aquarium, Penac P		*Anubias barteri* var. *barteri*	*Apistogramma trifasciata* "Guapore "
CO₂	/Original direct injection system		*Scindapsus* sp.	*Apistogramma ataphalpa*
Aeration	/Original aeration system	Animals	/*Hemiodopsis gracilis*	*Apistogramma* sp. "Breitbinden"
Additives	/Brighty K; Green Brighty STEP 2; ECA; Green Gain		*Paracheirodon axelrodi*	*Apistogramma juruensis*
Water Change	/Automatic water change system		*Paracheirodon simulans*	*Caridina japonica*
Water Quality	/Temperature 75°F; pH 6.8; TH 20mg/l		*Aplochelichtys normanni*	*Otocinclus* sp.

AMANO MAGIC

A few years ago an American magazine published a photograph of an aquarium that I produced with *Pterophyllum scalare* with a title of "AMANO MAGIC." The caption for it read "No, this isn't an underwater photo taken in the Amazon. This gorgeous school of altum angels *Pterophyllum altum* swims peacefully in a Nature Aquarium designed and maintained by famed aquascaping master Takashi Amano."

During a presentation I gave in Atlanta last year, I showed many slides of Nature Aquarium and said "I don't think that you would have doubted that these were photographs of underwater scenery if you did not know the truth." Everybody in the audience looked like they agreed with me.

It is rather simple to trick people as this indicates. If you wish to become a first class aquarist, you have to be able to do at least that much. But if you wish to be topnotch, you must be able to trick fish. Of course, the fish must be wild caught individuals from the Amazon, West Africa, or Southeast Asia. You would be topnotch if you could trick these fish into thinking that they were back in their home water. This is the difference between the first class and the topnotch in my opinion.

I would like to create a paradise for fish through Nature Aquarium.

Epilogue
Continuing to Create Nature Aquarium

● The Idea of Nature Aquarium

Brilliant, circular air bubbles, rich in oxygen, which adorn the leaves of aquatic plants, are a sign of a properly functioning ecosystem in an aquarium. Ever since the day I discovered that adding CO_2 to water makes aquatic plants photosynthesize vigorously, these bubbles became an important signal for judging the condition of aquatic plants and, therefore, an overall Nature Aquarium condition. Fish swim around actively in a well-balanced environment. Some may stake their territories and chase other fish, and others may engage in courtship behavior and display beautiful nuptial colors. As demonstrated by the symbiosis between the roots of aquatic plants and root nodule bacteria in the soil, an ecosystem of beneficial microorganisms, called microflora, exists in every beautiful aquarium. As long as this ecosystem functions well, the beautiful environment can be sustained. Aquatic plants and countless microorganisms purify the water and convert CO_2 into oxygen through photosynthesis, and new generations of fish will continue to emerge. On the other hand, if the quantity of aquatic plants is too small, the environment in the aquarium cannot be sustained. The aquarium will sustain huge damages if the water temperature increases. The amount of carbon dioxide should not be too big or too little. The relationship between the environment and living organisms that can be seen in an aquarium is a miniature version of the ecosystems on Earth. Although the Earth sustains many lives in an exquisite balance, a disruption in the balance will result in huge problems. A planted aquarium teaches us this mechanism.

I wanted to have an aquarium with densely growing aquatic plants in the first place because I thought that it was normal for fish to have aquatic plants in their environment. When I was a child, kids used to dive and catch fish in a nearby river and lagoon for fun. We always saw the bushes of aquatic plants where fish run and hide. The scenery and the sensations that were captured using all five senses as well as my yearning for undulating aquatic plants and beautifully shining fish are etched in my mind as vivid memories. Fish are said to use aquatic plants not only because their stems and leaves offer a hiding place and a spawning place, but also because there is an abundant amount of oxygen around the aquatic plants, and the plants give off antiseptic substances against bacteria and algae. Additionally, leaves and roots of aquatic plants actively absorb nitrogen from water and purify the water around them. Therefore, fish and their eggs can stay healthy there. A bare tank that was once popular looked to me like a cage to lock up fish. Without being taught by anybody, I simply wanted to recreate a near-natural environment to keep fish in.

Growing aquatic plants in an aquarium was not very popular at that time. It was like groping in the dark initially. I started out with popular types of plants, such as *Hygrophila polysperma* and *Echinodorus amazonicus*. As I established a method to grow aquatic plants gradually by developing substrate materials, liquid fertilizers, CO_2 injection system, and lighting systems, the types of aquatic plants that I could grow also increased gradually, and eventually the plants grew densely in my aquariums. I started taking photographs of aquariums to keep records of the layouts that I created. Doing so made me even more conscious of the compositional beauty of a layout. Today's

Nature Aquarium that integrates the concept of ecosystem, and natural beauty was established from there. At the same time, I visited many places, not only in Japan, but also in the world, such as the Amazon, West Africa, and Southeast Asia, searching for the natural habitats of aquatic plants and fish and unexplored places of nature that I can use as references for layouts. What I gained in these places was not only knowledge of the growing environment of aquatic plants and fish, but also inspiring experiences and experiences that shook my heart greatly, such as the thrill of witnessing majestic sceneries that mother nature created, and the sadness and confusion that I felt toward the current global environmental conditions. These experiences were a big influence on my layout style. Creating Nature Aquarium and photographing nature are connected and inseparable in my mind.

● The significance of taking photographs with large format films

All of the aquascape pictures that are contained in this photo book were taken with large format films. Sizes of the films range from 8 x 20, 11 x 14, 8 x10, 5 x 7, to 4 x 5 inches. I use 8 x 10 inch films primarily for photographing aquariums. The use of a 4 x 5 inch film is limited to taking photographs of mini aquariums. I also use 8 x 20 inch format films for a 11.5-ft- or 8-ft-long aquarium with a wide aspect ratio. (8 x 20 inch format films are custom-made specifically for me by Fuji Film.) As this indicates, I use various, large format films for taking aquascape photographs, depending on the size and aspect ratio of an aquarium. A characteristic of a large format film is its tremendously large area as compared to normal 35 mm films. A 4 x 5

inch format film, which is the smallest one of them all, has an area approximately 13 times the size of a 35 mm film. An 8 x 10 inch format film is about 56 times as big, and an 8 x 20 inch format film, the largest one, is about 110 times as big. The larger the size of a film becomes, the smaller the decline will be in the picture quality when printed as a part of printed matter. Since the image from a 35 mm film is normally blown up for printing, the image quality becomes degraded, or the image will not be very sharp. A large format film does not have to be blown up as much and is often scaled down instead. The color reversal films (primarily Fujichrome Velvia and Velvia 100F) that I used for the photographs have vibrant colors and extremely fine granularity. Therefore, the film can capture an image vividly in detail, all the way to every corner of an aquarium. The purpose of taking aquascape photographs is to keep records of produced layouts. The types of aquatic plants and fish can be identified if the photographs are taken with a large format film. Since aquatic plants in a layout keep on growing, the aquascape keeps changing everyday as well. There is no better method than a large format film to precisely capture the most beautiful instance of the layout.

However, the type of camera that can use large format films is limited to large format cameras with flexible bellows. Its operation is quite unique as compared to standard SLR cameras. Its use is limited to very specialized applications, such as architectural photography and the reproduction of works of art, and therefore not many people use them. As for the operating style, a photographer will use a dark cloth called a focusing cloth over his head and focus an image by looking

at a dark, ground glass with a loupe. The image on the ground glass is upside down and in reverse from side to side. The four corners of the image are very dim and therefore a certain skill is required to decide on the composition. The tilt, which is an operation specific to a large format camera with bellows, and the exposure compensation with bellows factors are also necessary. The exposure is set by manually adjusting the diaphragm and the shutter speed based on the value measured with an exposure meter. Everything must be operated manually. It is a photography style in the ultimate analog form. I bought enough books on large format cameras to fill two carton boxes in the used books district in Kanda, Tokyo, and I learned the shooting techniques on my own. Although the writing in the books looked like a bunch of foreign words in the beginning, I began to get a vague idea after studying them feverishly for a week. A year later, I was knowledgeable enough to give a lecture on the subject. A large format camera and its lenses were extremely expensive by themselves, but they weren't the only things that were necessary. It is necessary to close the aperture down to extend the depth of field (the range of acceptable sharpness.) However, closing down the aperture causes the shutter speed to be extremely slow under the light for an aquarium and this blurs the image of fish. Since light diminishes in water quickly, a blinding amount of light must be flashed for an instance with many large studio strobe lights to capture the image of fish with the aperture closed down. Since more than ten 3200W strobe lights are used to shoot a 6 ft aquarium, they periodically trip a breaker. Because I would like to preserve a layout that I create in a photograph and have the beautiful aquascape seen by as many people as possible, I insist on large format films and will go to such lengths. Since an actual Nature Aquarium is not easy to transport and its condition changes from one day to the next, the number of people who can actually see it in person is quite limited. Although we have the Nature Aquarium Gallery now, there wasn't any place that could display many layouts all together back then. Therefore, I took advantage of photographs and publications to the fullest. Aided by the vivid aquascape pictures that were published in aquarium magazines and photo books, Nature Aquarium spread all over Japan and then overseas.

● Always Being Conscious of Nature

It is true that my interest in nature deepened as I continued to

create Nature Aquarium and produce aquascape pictures. I was taking landscape photographs in the past, and they came in handy for designing compositions and rendering a natural feel to a layout in Nature Aquarium. As I watch beautiful nature deteriorate at locations where I once took photographs, I could not overlook the shadow of environmental problems. During the past fifteen years, I traveled to not only various parts of Japan, but also the three largest tropical rainforests of the Amazon, Borneo, and West Africa, carrying my large format cameras to take pictures. I devoted myself more and more to taking photographs because I was driven by the mounting frustrations that I would never be able to photograph the scenery again unless I took it then, since the environmental destruction that was caused by logging and burning of the forests was worsening at an alarming speed.

I was also frustrated by the superficial conservationism at times. Tropical fish are quite popular in the world now and there is a high demand for them. The number of tropical fishes is said to have declined drastically due to frequent overexploitations by poachers and outsiders. The government of Brazil imposed a severe restriction on the export of tropical fishes due to the protest of a certain animal rights organization. As a result, local

people who made a living by collecting and selling tropical fishes lost their jobs and had to turn to slash-and-burn agriculture and logging for livelihood. I have taken aerial and underwater photographs in addition to landscape photographs in the Amazon. I witnessed a vast area of tropical rainforests being lost, and the beautiful, white sand beach along the Negro river basin got covered up by ashes from the slash-and-burn agriculture, diminishing to a mere shadow of what it used be over the course of a few years. An encounter with scenery is said to be a once-in-a-lifetime thing. Not only can we not see the same scenery again because of the passing times, but in recent years we often cannot see the same scenery again physically because of human-induced environmental destructions. I started feeling like it was my mission to record the few remaining unexplored examples of nature in every detail with large format films. A similar thing is happening to nature in Japan as well. The familiar nature around us is disappearing every year. I am putting efforts into photographing natural landscapes in Japan lately. Living creatures are disappearing rapidly from nearby areas and the natural sceneries of rivers and mountains have changed greatly due to three sided revetments and power lines. One of my reasons for using large format films for taking aquascape photographs as well as landscape photographs was to record them. A large format film has a much larger area than a 35 mm film or a medium format film and can hold a tremendous amount of information. Therefore, a landscape photograph that is taken with a large format film can become a precise record, a record from which the types of trees and grass and the evidence of animal activities can be deciphered, unlike a simple landscape photograph taken by other films. I would like to leave them as records of nature that existed in the past which can be passed down from generation to generation to the children 100 years from now. These are records of natural environment and ecosystems. I call them ecological landscape photographs lately.

I am also working on a biotope development in the past 15 years in addition to photographing natural sceneries at home and abroad. The surrounding areas of my house and ADA headquarters, which are turned into Nature Biotope by planting many trees and underbrush, have gradually turned into havens, where not only countless insects and spiders but also field mice, frogs, snakes and pheasants congregate. Nature Aquarium that recreates nature in an aquarium and a biotope where living things congregate naturally embrace the same ideas at their foundation.

●**The power of continuous activities**

Looking back, I realize that I have been creating Nature Aquarium for more than half of my life. Perhaps I have been able to continue doing one thing for this long because I have held onto my principle of being continuously active. Our willingness to learn is sure to help us some day. Therefore, I always tell my staff to "act without hesitation." Taking action by using all five senses is the best thing to do when we are faced with something that we don't understand or we are worried about. Reading books or looking at a magnificent work

of art can also broaden our perspective. A broader perspective gained through various experiences can change the amount and quality of information that one obtains when looking at a natural landscape. I have learned many things from nature as I worked with Nature Aquarium. Every little thing, such as the position of rocks and the way grass grows around them, driftwood washed onto the shore and the way that ferns and mosses are growing on it, the flow of water and the presence of living things, a pain or a sensation on my skin, an exhilarating feeling that I got, are all taken in and capitalized upon in the production of my layouts. I basically consider Nature Aquarium an outdoor hobby. Although it is placed indoors, its inspirations and materials for a layout are lying around in nature. I have provided as much various information as possible in a layout that I gained through actual experiences. I hope that viewers can sense the drama of the majestic nature behind it and take an interest in the real nature from there. The effect of man-induced environmental destruction and global warming on ecosystems is getting more serious every year. I believe that we can cure the disease of environmental problems that has spread across the globe if each of us takes an interest in nature and becomes conscious of the problems. In order to get as many people as possible interested in nature, I will continue to take photographs of nature and create Nature Aquarium layouts.

Takashi Amano

Born in Niigata, Japan in 1954. Conducted a research on the growing methodology of water plants on his own and established his original planted aquarium style, "Nature Aquarium." With the concept, "One who cannot love her smallest creations, cannot claim to stand before Nature" his aquarium layouts which combine the beauty of nature and mechanism of ecosystem have been introduced in aquarium magazines and highly praised domestically and internationally. In 1982, he established Aqua Design Amano Co., Ltd. Since then, he has been developing products "Nature Aquarium Goods," which are related to planted aquarium with high quality and stylish design, and promoting Nature Aquarium. Those products developed based on his personal experience such as lighting system for growing water plants, "NA Lamp," CO_2 supply equipment, "Pollen Glass," substrate, "Aqua Soil" made growing water plants dramatically easier and created a sensational hit in aquarium industry. In 1992, he published his collection of works in "Glass no Naka no Daishizen," followed by "Mizu-Shizen eno Kaiki," both of which were translated in 5 languages and published around the world. Photographs in those books were taken by Amano himself using large format cameras, and crisp descriptions keeps fascinating hobbyists around the world until today. To pursue inspirations for creating a layout, he has been taking photographs of world's three largest tropical rain forests (Amazon, Borneo, and West Africa) using large format cameras. Also as an environmental photographer, he works actively by giving lectures and organizing exhibitions. In recent years, he has established the International Environment Photographers Association (IEPA) and organizes exhibitions to enlighten the environmental awareness through environmental photographs.

International Environment Photographers Association (IEPA) President
Japan Professional Photographers Society (JPS)
Japan Advertising Photographers' Association (APA) Members
Society of Scientific Photography (SSP) Member

Bibliography

Year	Title	Publisher
1992	"Glass no Naka no Daishizen"	Marine Planning
1994	"Mizu-Shizen eno Kaiki"	Marine Planning
	"Nature Aquarium World"	TFH Publications
	"Pflanzenparadies unter Wasser"	Natur Buch Verlag
1996	"Nature Aquarium World Book 2"	TFH Publications
	"Nature Aquarium World Book 3"	TFH Publications
	"De wonderlijke wereld onder water"	Natur Design Verlag
	"Faszinierendes Aquarium"	Natur Buch Verlag
	"Le Nouveau Monde des Plantes Aquatiques"	Natur Design Verlag
1997	"Aquarium Plant Paradises"	TFH Publications
	"Aquari Zen"	Editoriale Giorgio Mondadori
	"Amanos Naturaquarien"	Bede Verlag
1998	"Ihr Hobby-Naturaquarien"	Bede Verlag
	"Diskus im Naturaquarium"	Bede Verlag
	"Das Große Buch der Naturaquarien"	Bede Verlag
	"Les aquariums naturels d'Amano"	JEH Productions
2004	"The Rio Negro"	Marine Planning
2007	"SADO - To Pristine Forest From Bottom of Sea"	ADA
2009	"SADO - To Pristine Forest From Bottom of Sea" Revised and Enlarged Edition	ADA
2010	"The Last Amazon"	Shogakukan

Layout Design/Photography:
Takashi Amano

Art Direction:
Takashi Sekiya

Editing of Japanese Edition:
Masatoshi Abe
Tsuyoshi Oiwa
Eriko Sekine
Yuka Hachinohe

Design:
Tetsuya Takahashi
Satoshi Maruyama
Ryo Ichikawa
Wataru Yanagibashi
Takanori Murata

Portrait Photography:
Yoshinori Watabe

English Translation:
Tomoko Schum

TFH Publications
President/CEO: Glen S. Axelrod
Executive Vice President: Mark E. Johnson
Editor-in-Chief: Albert Connelly, Jr.
Production Manager: Kathy Bontz
English Edition Editors: David Boruchowitz and Thomas Mazorlig

TFH Publications, Inc.
One TFH PlazaThird and Union Avenues
Neptune City, NJ 07753

Printed and bound in China
13 14 15 16   3 5 7 9 8 6 4

Library of Congress Cataloging-in-Publication Data
Amano, Takashi.
   Nature aquarium : complete works, 1985-2009 / Takashi Amano.
   p. cm.
   ISBN 978-0-7938-0649-2 (alk. paper)
  1. Aquatic plants. 2. Aquatic plants--Pictorial works. 3. Aquariums.
4. Aquariums--Pictorial works. I. Title.
   SF457.7.A474 2011
   635.9'674--dc22
                                                    2010039335

This book has been published with the intent to provide accurate and authoritative information in regard to the subject matter within. While every reasonable precaution has been taken in preparation of this book, the author and publisher expressly disclaim responsibility for any errors, omissions, or adverse effects arising from the use or application of the information contained herein. The techniques and suggestions are used at the reader's discretion and are not to be considered a substitute for veterinary care. If you suspect a medical problem consult your veterinarian.

The Leader In Responsible Animal Care For Over 50 Years!